POCKET
BOOKS

## ALSO BY DR BOB ROTELLA

*Golf Is Not a Game of Perfect*
*Golf Is a Game of Confidence*
*The Golf of Your Dreams*
*Putting Out of Your Mind*
*Life Is Not a Game of Perfect*

# THE GOLFER'S MIND

## Play to Play Great

o o o

## DR BOB ROTELLA

WITH **Bob Cullen**

POCKET
BOOKS

LONDON • SYDNEY • NEW YORK • TORONTO

This edition first published in Great Britain by Pocket Books, 2007
An Imprint of Simon & Schuster UK Ltd
A CBS COMPANY

Copyright © Robert J. Rotella, 2004

7 9 10 8 6

Simon & Schuster UK Ltd
1st Floor
222 Gray's Inn Road
London WC1X 8HB

www.simonandschuster.co.uk

Simon & Schuster Australia
Sydney

A CIP catalogue record for this book is available
from the British Library

ISBN 13: 978-1-4165-0229-6

Printed and bound in Great Britain by
CPI Cox & Wyman, Reading, RG1 8EX

*To the memory of Davis Love, Jr.*

*Thanks to my wife, Darlene, and my daughter, Casey,
who offer so much support and
give so freely of their time.*

# CONTENTS

O O O

# INTRODUCTION

# MY TOP TEN

O  O  O

*All of the rings and all of the money and all of the
color and display—they linger only in memory. The
spirit, the will to win and excel, these are the things
that endure. The quality of any man's life is the full
measure of his commitment to excellence and to
victory, regardless of what field he might be in.*
—Vince Lombardi

I teach the psychology of greatness. The way I teach it varies.

When I first begin to work with a client, I like to arrange for
him or her to come to my home in Virginia. We spend a couple
of days together, some of it in conversation and some of it on
the golf course. I get to know the client thoroughly. He is immersed in my ideas about using the mind to achieve greatness,

about playing to play great, about bringing the best possible attitude to play and practice.

After that, the nature of my contact with my clients may change. Some of them still like to come to Virginia periodically for a long session. But others prefer shorter talks on specific issues and problems that have arisen in their careers. I might meet them for lunch or dinner in a town that's hosting a golf tournament. We might chat on the putting green or the practice range. Sometimes we talk over the phone while he's in a hotel room and I'm at an airport.

This book is akin to that second category of counseling sessions. In fact, it arises partly from them. When I talk to a player who says, "Doc, I'm having trouble trusting my swing," I review the fundamental ideas about the necessity of trust and why it helps a golfer produce the best shots he's capable of making. Players have often wished I had a book, a handbook if you will, that could serve the same function and reinforce those conversations. This is that book.

If you're completely unfamiliar with sports psychology as I teach it and with its application to golf, you might want to consult one of my earlier books, like *Golf Is Not a Game of Perfect.* It's my primer on how great golfers think.

Often what I hear from readers of those earlier books is something to the effect that, "Your ideas were really helpful right after I read them, Doc, but lately they don't seem to work well." What that tells me is not that the ideas have gotten less effective. It tells me that over time, the reader has forgotten some of them. Or he's reverted to old ways of thinking, perhaps without realizing it.

This doesn't surprise me. The players with whom I work individually are prone to the same problem. If the issue is trusting the swing for instance, they might be able to do it very well in the months after we have our initial session. It's one of the things I stress. But over time, a golfer is exposed to a barrage of contradictory ideas. People are telling him to think about the way his hands cock the club or the ratio between his hip turn and his shoulder turn. If he's a professional, he gets this sort of advice from renowned instructors on the practice range at Tour venues. If he's an average player, he gets it from magazines and television. Pretty soon, instead of trusting his swing and thinking about his target, he's thinking about pronation while he's on the golf course. He's trying to swing while his mind sorts through bits and pieces of conflicting advice. That's difficult to do.

When this happens with one of my established clients, I review the essentials with him. This book is an effort to do the same thing for readers. It's a distilled version of what I teach.

So often, in those telephone sessions, I return to ten fundamental points of good golf thinking. If Moses hadn't already copyrighted the name, I would be tempted to call them my ten commandments for playing great golf. I know that if a player adheres to them, he can find out exactly how low his skills are prepared to take him on any given round. Here they are:

I.  **Play to play great. Don't play not to play poorly.**

II.  **Love the challenge of the day, whatever it may be.**

III.  **Get out of results and get into process.**

**IV.** Know that nothing will bother or upset you on the golf course, and you will be in a great state of mind for every shot.

**V.** Playing with a feeling that the outcome doesn't matter is almost always preferable to caring too much.

**VI.** Believe fully in yourself so you can play freely.

**VII.** See where you want the ball to go before every shot.

**VIII.** Be decisive, committed, and clear.

**IX.** Be your own best friend.

**X.** Love your wedge and your putter.

These ideas may sound obscure or strange to you. If you finish reading this book, they won't. I intend to explain each of them, and by the time I'm done, you will understand why they're so important. I hope you'll want to re-read them often.

The first person who suggested the format for this book to me was the late Davis Love, Jr. He and I worked together on the staff of Golf Digest Schools before his tragic death in a plane crash in 1988. He told me once that he wished there was a book of instruction on the mental side of golf, broken down into topics. He thought that a player could carry the book with him or keep it close by. When he needed to refresh his thinking about a particular issue, he could consult the book, read it for a few minutes, and come away with sound advice aimed at his problem. Not only do I owe the idea behind this book to Davis Love, Jr., I owe him so much more. He taught me a lot about golf, and he was a great friend. That's why the book is dedicated to him.

I hope readers will use this book as Davis Love, Jr., envisioned. You might want to read it in its entirety first. After your first consultation, I intend the book to be available as a handbook. You may want to consult some chapters, like "A Golfing Philosophy" on a regular basis, because it's so easy to lose track of the fundamental ideas in that chapter. If you're getting ready for a tournament and you feel the need for some advice on putting, for example, or acceptance, or game plan, you can go right to the chapters on those topics. Read as much as you need. Use the thoughts at the end of each chapter for a quick refresher. Put the book aside and come back to it when you need it again.

Sometimes people ask me if I teach psychological "techniques." I don't. The word "technique" suggests to me some sort of mental parlor trick. I don't want you to have faith in a technique. I want you to have faith in yourself. Your mind can be a powerful tool that will help you realize your dreams and aspirations. But you have to control it and use it properly. You have to coach yourself. You have to believe in yourself.

What I teach is both simple and difficult. It's simple, for instance, to say that you have to be committed before you start your swing, that doubt and indecision can ruin a shot. But on the course, it's not so easy to be committed. It takes discipline and practice.

The fact that it's hard is one reason it's worthwhile. Having control of your mind and using it properly can separate you from the competition, whether it's at your club or on the PGA Tour.

I believe that virtually every golfer has the potential to be much better than he or she is, and that using the mind is one essential way to improve. You will never know if you have the ability to be the best player in the world, or the best player in your club, unless you commit yourself to developing both your physical and mental skills. This book can be part of that commitment.

"Commitment" can be an imposing word. It can suggest that using your mind properly is an onerous chore, that you might shoot lower scores, but enjoy the game less. Trust me. The players I know who have the best minds also have the most fun playing golf. They understand that it is, in the end, a game. They have a ball finding out how good they can be at it.

So can you.

## THOUGHTS TO PLAY BY

Play to play great. Don't play not to play poorly.

Love the challenge of the day, whatever it may be.

Get out of results and get into process.

Know that nothing will bother or upset you on the golf course, and you will be in a great state of mind for every shot.

Playing with a feeling that the outcome doesn't matter is almost always preferable to caring too much.

Believe fully in yourself so you can play freely.

See where you want the ball to go before every shot.

Be decisive, committed, and clear.

Be your own best friend.

Love your wedge and your putter.

# ONE

# A GOLFING PHILOSOPHY

O O O

*The greatest pleasure is obtained by improving.*
—*Ben Hogan*

Why does my first session with a player usually last two days? I take this much time in part because I prefer not to jump right into a discussion of the particular problem that brought the player to me. I like to have a general discussion of the client's and my own basic ideas about the game of golf. In my less modest moments, I think of these ideas as a philosophy of the game.

I don't care if my client thinks of them as a philosophy or merely as a set of ideas. I do care whether he or she subscribes to them. If we can't come to agreement on these fundamental principles, it's much less likely that I can help the client. If we do see the game in roughly the same way, it becomes much easier to solve the specific issue that's troubling the player.

To begin with, I believe golf is a game of both confidence and competence. I am not about to tell anyone that a player who lacks physical skills can transform himself overnight into a winner by changing his thinking. If you trust a bad swing, it's still going to produce bad shots. (Though it will produce fewer of them than it will if you don't trust it.) You have to attain a level of physical competence to play well.

Having said that, though, I believe it's impossible to overestimate the importance of the mind in golf. There is no such thing as "muscle memory." Your muscles have no capacity to remember anything. Memory resides in your head. Therefore, no matter how long you practice a golf swing, no matter how skilled you become at it, your muscles alone can't remember it and execute it when the need arises on the golf course. Your muscles and the rest of your body are controlled by your mind. Unless your mind is functioning well when you play golf, your muscles are going to flounder. If your head is filled with bad thoughts, your scorecard is going to be full of bad strokes.

I'm not sure, actually, where the body ends and the mind begins, and I don't believe anyone is. I don't know where the soul and the spirit are located in a human being, but I know they exist. I think it's more useful to consider a human being, and a golfer, as a seamless organism. Your golf swing will not work well if it employs only the torso and not the legs. The torso and the legs are part of an integrated system, and all the parts of that system have to function in order to hit a golf ball. In the same way, what we refer to for the sake of convenience as your body and your mind are in reality parts of an integrated system. All the parts of that system must function properly in order to play golf well.

Golf is a game. It's not a science experiment that can be completed in accordance with immutable physical laws. It's not a jigsaw puzzle where the pieces are designed to fit together and yield a perfect picture. It's a game, and it must be played.

Because it's a game played by human beings on God's green earth, golf is a game of mistakes and unpredictable fortune. If it were not, no one would ever miss a fairway, a green, or a putt. On top of that, there would be no sudden gusts of wind, no unfortunate bounces, no imperfections in the turf. Every ball would go exactly where you wanted it to go, and the winning score in a golf tournament would be something like 50 strokes per round.

If you truly love golf, you must love the fact that no one shoots 50, that golf is an inherently imperfect game. If you spend your time fighting the fact that golf is a game of mistakes and trying to make it a game of perfect shots, you're really saying that you don't like golf. You want it to be some other game—billiards, maybe. No one has ever perfected golf—not Ben Hogan, not Jack Nicklaus, not Annika Sorenstam. I don't believe anyone ever will.

The players I see trying to force perfection into golf don't look to me as if they're having a very good time. They think that when they finally get the game down perfectly, they'll be recognized and adored for it. I envision them as 90-year-olds, still wondering when the game will come together perfectly. In the meantime, they've played countless rounds with scowls on their faces. They walk off the course looking frightened, unhappy, frustrated—looking like anything but an individual who's just spent four or five hours playing a beloved game. They look like they've just stepped out of a Siberian prison camp instead of a golf course.

These might be people who will spend hours talking about

how much they love the game. But when they get honest about their feelings, they'll admit that while they might love reading about golf, swapping stories about golf, even practicing golf, they don't actually love playing golf, at least not while they're doing it. After a round, they're still consumed by tension and anxiety. They're unpleasant to be with.

If this is your attitude toward golf, why would you make it your hobby? Still more, why would you make it your profession?

Golfers who truly understand and love the game accept it, rather than fight it. They realize that the essence of golf is reacting well to its inevitable mistakes and misfortunes. They know that they can separate themselves from their competition, not by perfecting their games, but by constantly striving to improve and reacting well to mistakes. I remind players that if there's one thing they should always be proud of in their golf games, it's how well they react to mistakes. I tell them that they will never have complete control of the golf ball. But they can control their attitudes.

The biggest mistake most people make is to respond passively to what happens on the golf course. They let how they play dictate their attitude. If the ball is going where they want it to go, they have a good attitude. If it isn't, their attitude is bad. They start thinking badly. When you're playing well, it's fine to go with the flow. But when you're playing badly, you need the discipline to control your thoughts and think only about the way you want to play.

Mastering this concept goes a long way in determining two critical outcomes. One is how good a player is going to get at golf. The second is how much fun he'll have along the way.

Golfers who have fun along the way understand that golf is first a game you play within yourself. You win that game by resisting all the mental temptations and pitfalls I'll be discussing in more detail later in this book. You win it by bringing both your mind and your body to bear on the test of golf as well as you possibly can.

Golf is the most honest of games in that you can't lie to yourself about how well you're doing in that personal game. The great players I work with are usually brutally honest about what went on in their minds during a round. I sometimes have happy professional clients talk to me after they've shot 75. Of course, they understand that 75 isn't a good score for a professional golfer. But they're happy with the way they played. By "the way they played," I don't mean how many strokes they took. I mean that they're happy with the attitude they maintained during the round, with their concentration, their focus, their thoughts. A player can control those things. He can't control his score.

Conversely, I've had clients shoot 65 and tell me very candidly that they were exceedingly lucky to do so. It can happen for a round or two. Maybe a player gets good bounces. Maybe he sinks some putts with less-than-trusting strokes because he misread the green. For a round or two, a player might get away with thinking poorly, but he knows that it will catch up with him. So it's quite possible that a player who shot 75 will be cheerfully optimistic about his game, and a player who shot 65 might be concerned.

I'm particularly impressed when this happens because another part of my philosophy is that a player is not the number at the bottom of his scorecard. A player's worth as a person is not directly correlated to the score he or she shoots. A golfer whose mood and self-esteem are determined by the score he shoots for a given round or tournament has a very superficial approach to both life and golf. On the other hand, a player has to care enough about the scores he shoots to want to practice and improve. Otherwise, he's wasting my time and his money talking to me.

I want players to understand that while it's important to have dreams and goals in golf, the pleasure comes from chasing those dreams more than it does from catching them. I can't guarantee any player that his dreams will come true. I can't predict when they'll come true. What I can guarantee is that a life spent chasing dreams is a life well spent. Anyone who does this will get to the end of his days and look back with a smile. He will have had a ball. Once a player understands this, it gives him remarkable peace of mind. He can weather the inevitable downs in a game of ups and downs. He doesn't get critical or judgmental about himself. He knows that in the end, things will turn out well. He's an optimist.

There's a difference between chasing dreams and daydreaming. Daydreamers sit on the couch and think that it would be nice to be winning tournaments, or scoring in the 70s. But they do nothing about it from one round of golf to the next. Consequently, they never improve. There's no satisfaction in that.

Golf is full of fine lines and balances. The idea that you mustn't define yourself by your golf score, but at the same time must care about it and want to improve it, is one example. Another is the balance between being a sponge and being bullheaded.

The sponge is a golfer who listens to anyone and everyone who wants to offer advice about his game. One week he's convinced that the action of the hands is the key to greatness. The next week it's the ratio between his shoulder turn and hip turn. Pretty soon, the sponge is so full of conflicting ideas that he can barely start the club back. He's thinking too hard, trying to sort out all the advice he's gotten.

The bullheaded player doesn't listen to anyone. He's uncoachable. He's been doing it a particular way for a long time and he likes doing it that way, even if he rarely breaks 90.

A successful golfer has to find a balance between the two extremes. You have to be true to your unique personality and skills, to relish the quirks that set you apart from others. You've got to love doing things your way. You have to love your talent and your game more than you love anyone else's. But you have to be amenable to improving your game. To be a great golfer, it's very important that you're self-reliant and have the ability to function independently, make decisions for yourself, and trust your instincts. But in order to get to greatness, you're going to have to surround yourself with some good people, people who will offer advice and help. On the amateur level it might be a club pro whom you respect, and trust, and make the only teacher you listen to for help on your swing. On the professional level it might be Butch Harmon or David Leadbetter. You're going to have to learn that there's a time to listen to such people and a time to be self-reliant. You'll have to learn the difference.

You must take responsibility for the talent you have. I dislike it when someone says to me, "I don't have the talent to be

No. 1." I dislike it just as much when someone says he hasn't got the talent to win his club championship or to have a single-digit handicap, or to break 90. The fact is, we don't know exactly how much talent anyone has. Talent is a mixture of physical and mental qualities that is immeasurable. When people think of golf talent, they think of Annika Sorenstam. But I don't know how physically talented Annika is. It's no knock on her to observe that I don't know of any other sport she's great at. She's great at golf because she devoted her time and energy to it, obviously. Whether she could have gotten great at any other endeavor is something we may never learn.

The question is not whether you have great talent, because we'll never answer that definitively. The question is whether you're willing to put in the time and energy to develop the talent you have. Sometimes a player will tell me that "If I had Tiger's (or Phil's or Davis's) talent to go along with my attitude, I'd be awesome." I always disagree. I disagree because I believe a great attitude includes loving your talent above anyone else's. It's part of the foundation of a great attitude.

You must also find a balance in your life. I know very few people who manage to keep their lives in any sort of rigid, systematic balance. I smile when someone tells me he's got his life broken down into blocks: eight hours for sleep, eight hours for work, four hours for family, three hours for golf, and maybe an hour for working out. Real people are always out of balance in some way. Maybe one month they're so immersed in work that they don't find enough time for their families, their golf, their fitness. But they recognize the imbalance and correct it the next month. Maybe the period of imbalance is much longer—measured in years, rather than weeks or months. It's fine for an aspiring professional to devote five, seven, or ten years to improving his golf game and establishing himself on the Tour, almost to the exclusion of all else. But at some point, the balance must be redressed.

On the golf course, there's a fine line between playing to play great and playing recklessly. A reckless player hits his driver off virtually every tee. He fires at sucker pins he has no business aiming at because he's convinced that's what playing to play great is all about. It isn't. A player who's playing to play great loves a great drive more than he fears the rough. He likes making putts more than he cares about three-putting. He loves chipping it in more than he loathes not getting up and down. But he may have a conservative strategy for certain holes. The conservative strategy is what permits him to always make a confident, even cocky swing. When the moment is right, when he's got a scoring club in his hands, he takes dead aim at the hole. But only when the moment is right.

The player who plays to play great understands that good can be the enemy of great. He knows that if he gets too concerned about not being bad, he might not free himself up enough to be great. He doesn't care very much about making cuts or Top 20 finishes. He plays to win.

If he does this, he controls his destiny as a golfer. I want clients to understand this. They have free will. The choices they make with that free will determine the quality of their golf game and the quality of their lives. If you consistently make the right choices, you're destined for greatness. I'm not suggesting that this necessarily means you're going to win all the Grand

Slam tournaments or all your club events, or even all your Saturday morning Nassaus. I'm saying that if you make the right choices, you will someday look back on your life, or that part of your life that was devoted to golf, and say, "Wow! That was great."

## THOUGHTS TO PLAY BY

Golf is a game, and it must be played.

Let your mind control the ball. Don't let the ball control your mind. You may not always control the ball, but you can always control your attitude.

Love your talent and your game more than you love anyone else's.

Good can be the enemy of great. Always play to play great.

Improve by working on both your physical skills and your mind, because golf is a game of both confidence and competence.

There is no such thing as 'muscle memory.'

If you truly love golf, you must love its inherent imperfectability.

The essence of golf is reacting well to the game's inevitable mistakes and misfortunes.

The biggest mistake most people make is letting what happens on the golf course control their attitudes.

A player is not the number at the bottom of his scorecard.

The pleasure of the game comes from chasing dreams more than catching them.

You control your destiny.

# TWO

# A GOLFER'S SENSE OF SELF

O  O  O

*You've got to think like a winner to win.*
*—Sam Snead*

Some twenty-five years ago, early in my career as a sports psychologist, I was beginning to explore the links between what I had learned about the mind's role in team sports like basketball and football, and the mind's role in golf. Someone from *Golf Digest* heard me speak about attitude and basketball. He invited me to speak to the staff of the Golf Digest Schools about attitude and athletic performance. I agreed.

If I had been better informed about golf then, I might have been too intimidated to open my mouth. The staff I was addressing included the premier teachers in the game; some of them were great players as well: Cary Middlecoff, Paul Runyan, Bob Toski, Davis Love, Jr., Jim Flick, and Peter Kostis were in the group.

There was one name on the staff that even a nongolfer would recognize: Sam Snead. He was one of those personalities that transcends a particular game and becomes famous even among people who don't follow sports. I was warned that Snead might not take kindly to listening to a young Ph.D. expound about a game he'd been playing for six decades about as well as it had ever been played. In fact, someone from *Golf Digest* warned me that Snead might very well rip me to shreds. I was advised not to take it personally if he did.

I spoke for about an hour, and then opened the floor for questions. Snead's hand was the first to go up. I remember thinking, "Well, here goes."

"I really enjoyed that," Snead said. "I can't help but think about how many U.S. Opens I would have won if I'd had someone like you to talk to."

I looked carefully to make sure he wasn't setting me up. His face was open and sincere. I started to relax.

Snead related the famous story of how he lost the 1939 U.S. Open at Spring Mill, outside Philadelphia. In those days, there were no scoreboards. Snead came to the final holes knowing he was in contention, but not knowing exactly where he stood. The truth was that he could have made a bogey six on the 72nd hole and still beaten Byron Nelson by a stroke. But he thought he needed a birdie to win and a par to tie. He drove the ball into the rough. Instead of playing for a likely par and a certain bogey, he started taking unnecessary risks, Eventually, he made an eight. He decided thereafter that he was jinxed at the Open, and he never won one.

But it was something Snead said next that fascinates me and reveals a great deal about a golfer's psychology. I had mentioned in my talk that the biggest mistake many athletes make is that they passively respond to their experiences. When things are going well, they're optimistic and cheerful. The occasional mistake is immediately forgotten. But when things go badly, they react by thinking badly. They brood. They dwell on their mistakes. They compound whatever physical issues brought on their slump by persuading themselves that their problems are intractable.

Snead thought that was a brilliant observation, and he told this story to explain what he meant:

"When I was the dominant player in golf," he said, "I would go to bed every night and imagine myself playing a great round the next day. Sometimes I got through the whole round, but many nights I'd fall asleep somewhere between the 6th and the 12th holes. It didn't matter. Because I fell asleep thinking about playing great golf shots, I'd sleep like a log. I'd wake up refreshed and ready to go. I'd get into the hotel shower. In those days, a hot shower felt like a privilege, because I hadn't had hot water growing up. I'd stand under the water for what seemed like forever, and again I'd start imagining the great round I was going to play that day. Then I'd have a very slow, relaxed breakfast.

"After that, someone would drive me to the course. I'd get in the car and the driver would start telling me what a pleasure it was to meet me and what a privilege it was to drive me. He'd tell me how great I was. He might tell me about my last win or ask me questions about it.

"I'd get to the golf course and warm up—usually with a 9-iron and a pitching wedge. I might hit a few drives to finish the warm-up, hit a few chips and a few putts, but mostly it was 9-iron and pitching wedge, because they gave me a nice rhythm and I figured if I had a good rhythm, I'd be fine.

"Then I'd go to the tee and the announcer would introduce me and cite all my wins, or at least the major ones. I'd get a huge ovation. At that point, I'd be feeling so good about myself I'd just think about playing great that day. I had such peace of mind that it didn't matter how I started. I knew before the round ended, I'd be playing great.

"After the round, I'd do an interview or two where I'd talk to the writers about my great round. Then, usually, we'd be playing at a club where they had nice showers, and I'd stay under their shower quite a while. I'd replay the day's round in my head, but if there were holes I wasn't happy with, I'd imagine how I wanted to play them the next day. Then I'd forget about golf and go out to dinner and enjoy myself till it was time to go to bed. Life was that easy."

"Then when I started struggling, I worried about my putting. Then I worried about how I was going to play. It was like you were saying. My thinking was the exact opposite."

Everyone in the room was spellbound as Snead opened himself up this way. He had a reputation as a bit of a curmudgeon. But he was baring his soul.

"I'd get into bed at night worried about how I was playing, and I wouldn't sleep well," Snead went on. "When it was time to wake up, I'd feel tired, and I'd think, 'Is it already time to wake up?' I'd want to stay in bed longer. I'd find myself rushing through the shower and rushing through breakfast. I always felt like I was running late and starting in the shower I'd worry about my game. On the way to the golf course, if the driver didn't say something about how I was struggling (Snead's belief that he had the putting yips and his efforts to cope with them through new grips and putting styles were widely chronicled),

I'd say something about it. So we'd drive to the golf course talking about how I hadn't been playing very well.

"When I got to the golf course, I started spending more time hitting longer clubs and chipping and putting, because those were the parts of the game I was struggling with. On the first tee, when they announced my titles, I'd be hearing it, but it made me worry about embarrassing myself and hurting my reputation and letting people down. On the golf course, if I made a couple of mistakes, I started worrying about having a bad day instead of feeling like I was bound to start playing well. After the round was over, if I did an interview, I was explaining why I didn't play well. I wasn't as good at letting it go. When I went out to dinner, I might start complaining about my putting, or the golf course, even wondering whether to keep playing any more.

"So, I think we should listen to this young man," Snead concluded. "I think he's got some valid points."

With Snead's benediction, the group then had a great two-hour discussion and debate about the role of the mind in the game. For me personally, it was a turning point. If Snead had cut me off, dismissed me as an academic theorist with nothing to teach real golfers, I might never have gone on to the work I've done. With his blessing, I started working with the Golf Digest Schools staff. Some time later, Peter Kostis asked if I'd like to work with a few of his students—Tom Kite, Gary Koch and Roger Maltbie.

My new clients had some impressive successes. The first week I worked with Kite, he won at Doral, birdieing three of the last four holes to beat Jack Nicklaus. Koch won a few weeks later, and then Kite won again, and Maltbie won. I started working with Denis Watson, who had never won and needed to make $50,000 in seven weeks or lose his card and go home to Zimbabwe. He won two or three times in the next seven tournaments. Then I started working with Pat Bradley of the LPGA Tour, who won three majors in a single year. The word-of-mouth advertising generated by these clients enabled me to spend the next 20 years teaching and learning from the best golfers in the world.

Nothing that I've seen, heard or learned in those years is more important than the lesson contained in the story Sam Snead told. It's a lesson about a golfer's self-image, and his subconscious mind. It's about how the subconscious affects his play.

For the purposes of this discussion, I am going to greatly simplify what we know about the brain and the mind. I am going to divide the mind into two sections, the conscious and the subconscious. Your subconscious houses your images of yourself. You have an overall image. You've also got an image of yourself as a golfer. Your golfing self-image can be broken down further. You've got separate images of yourself as a driver, as a putter, as a chipper, and as a bunker player. You've got an image of yourself as a winner, or an also-ran. They're all important, because golf is a game best played by letting your subconscious govern your body. To play it well, you need a good image of yourself playing the shot at hand.

The subconscious works a bit like a computer program that does your tax return. In the case of the program, you enter data about your income and deductions. The program tells you how you stand with the government. The subconscious gets its input from the conscious mind. It absorbs all the thoughts you have about yourself. Like the tax program, it gives you a net assessment.

Also like the tax program, it is neither discerning nor selective. The tax program doesn't know whether the numbers you feed it are accurate. It doesn't care. It simply accepts the data it's given and calculates the result. The subconscious doesn't know whether the thoughts you feed to it are accurate, either. It simply accepts them. It can't edit your thoughts. Nor can it correct them.

At any given moment, your self-image is like a running total kept by your subconscious of the thoughts you've had about yourself. It's changed and updated every moment of every day. But here the analogy of the tax program breaks down. Your tax program doesn't weigh one input more than another. Your subconscious does. It gives more weight to recent thoughts than to older ones. It gives more weight to thoughts that were associated with strong emotions than to thoughts that were routine and humdrum.

You can now better see what Sam Snead was doing to himself in his good times and his bad times. When he was playing well, Snead's every thought contributed to a powerful self-image. From his dreams at night to his conversations on the way to the golf course, he fed his subconscious data that created an internal image of a great golfer. But when things started to go badly, Snead compounded his problem by dwelling on his poor shots. And Snead was a great player. He still holds the career record with 81 PGA Tour victories. If it was difficult for him to maintain a strong self-image, you can understand how difficult it can be for players with lesser records.

The subconscious tries to accommodate the conscious and give back what it thinks the conscious mind wants. Thus, as Snead brooded about his putting, his subconscious was forming a new image, the image of a man who got nervous and twitchy over short putts. Sure enough, he became more nervous and more twitchy.

You may think, "Well, Snead was just being realistic. He had a real problem with short putts."

Think again. Certainly, you can't say that Snead somehow lost the physical strength to hit short putts. His problem was mental. Like everyone else, he missed some short ones. Was it realistic to brood about the missed putts till he convinced himself he had a problem? Was it realistic then to compound the problem by more worrying and brooding? Or would it in fact have been realistic for Snead to recall and dwell on all the short putts he'd made, many in critical situations?

I suggest the latter.

Here's another analogy that may help explain how the subconscious and the self-image work. Think of your body. Assuming you're free of disease, its condition is a running total of inputs, the same way your subconscious self-image is a reflection of all the thoughts you've had about yourself. At this moment, your body's condition reflects all the decisions you've made about eating, drinking, and exercising. If you've been making good decisions, your body is in good shape. If, just as an example, someone offered you a million dollars to run from where you are now to a point six miles away in less than an hour, you could probably do it.

But if, at the moment, your body reflects a lifetime of overeating, overdrinking, and a lack of exercise, it wouldn't matter if someone offered you ten million dollars to cover six miles in sixty minutes. You'd want to, of course. You'd set out and try your best. But your body just wouldn't be able to do it.

It's the same way with your self-image. If you find yourself thrust into a tense, competitive situation, like being in contention on the last few holes of a tournament, you can't suddenly change your self-image. If your self-image says you have a tendency to hit balls into the water on tough holes, or a tendency to miss critical putts, that's what you're likely to do if you let the subconscious control your body.

The good news is that, like your physical fitness, you control your self-image. It's called your "self-image" because you create it yourself, with all the thoughts you have about yourself and your golf game.

You can improve your self-image. It can't happen instantly, any more than you could remake your body with a single day of exercise and sensible eating. But if you went on a good diet and followed an exercise plan for a year, your body would change. If you give your subconscious a steady stream of helpful thoughts for a sustained period of time and if you attach emotions like joy, pride, and satisfaction to your successes, you can change your self-image, just as a sustained diet and exercise regiment will change your body. Remember, the working principle here is that recent input is more influential than older input. But to begin, you have to change your thinking.

Greg Norman once told me a story that suggested how he fashioned his self-image. As a teenager in Australia, he felt destined to do great things with his life. He wasn't sure if it was going to be in golf or in business, but he felt destined. Around that time, there was a popular song with the lyrics, "Keep on singing, don't stop singing, you're going to be a star someday." That song lodged in Norman's brain, though he changed the lyrics when he sang it to himself as he practiced. His version was "Keep on swinging, don't stop swinging, you're going to be a star some day." He heard that tune in his head 500 times a day from the time he was fifteen until he became the number one player in the world.

If you want to be a winner, it helps enormously to see yourself as a winner, whether it's on the PGA Tour or in your Saturday Nassau. This is not to say that accidents can't happen. A player who doesn't see himself as a winner might occasionally back into a win. He might yank one into the woods and see it bounce back into the fairway. Or someone else might blow up over the final holes. But do you want to wait for that kind of luck, or do you want to control your destiny?

Our subconscious self-images act like thermostats. Just as a thermostat regulates the temperature in our homes, our subconscious self-images regulate us. Your home thermostat essentially defines an interior comfort zone, a temperature range that suits your home. If you set it at 70 degrees, and the temperature drops much below that, the heat will kick on and raise the temperature back into the comfort zone. If the temperature rises above 73 or so, the air conditioner will start and stay on until the temperature is back to 70.

On the golf course, the subconscious tries to keep us in what it perceives as our comfort zone. If a player sees himself as the sort who never shoots a big number but also can't go low, the subconscious will work to ensure that kind of score. If the player makes a few birdies early in the round and seems capable of shooting 65, the subconscious will try to engineer a few bogies to return the score for the day to the player's comfort zone. If he bogies a couple early, the subconscious will sharpen his focus until he makes some compensating birdies. Weekend players notice this same syndrome. How often has someone made a birdie and followed it with a bogey or a double bogey on the next hole? That's the subconscious trying to restore the comfort zone of a player who perceives himself as a bogey golfer.

This mechanism operates on several levels. It can influence a shot and a round. It can influence a season and a career. If a player perceives himself as the sort of golfer who wins once a year, his subconscious will work to create a let-down if he wins early in the year. If a player perceives himself as a Top 50 performer but not a Top 10 player, his subconscious will work over the course of his career to assure that outcome. On the other hand, a player who sees himself winning many tournaments, who perceives himself as the holder of major titles, will have a strong boost from his subconscious as he strives to realize his dreams.

Our self-image can change as we move into new environments. I taught for many years at the University of Virginia, which is a very selective, competitive school. I saw many students who had excelled in high school gradually persuade themselves that they were not as smart as they used to think they were. By the time they were in their third or fourth years, their subconscious perception had changed. They saw themselves as mediocre students, or failing students. Seeing themselves that way, they performed that way. The same thing can happen to a great amateur golfer, a collegiate star, when he or she moves up to professional golf. They have to work hard to maintain the self-image they had as amateurs. They have to work at it just as much as they do on their physical skills.

Physical skills, by the way, are obviously important, and I'm not suggesting that perceiving yourself as a winner is sufficient to becoming a winner. As I've said, golf is a game of both competence and confidence, and a player without the requisite skills can't win. But the reality is that there are plenty of players who do have the requisite skills, but don't win. This is why.

Most people either aren't aware that they have a subconscious self-image, or they perceive it only dimly. Very few understand that they can affect it. Most of us are like Sam Snead was, reacting passively to what we do and to what we are told. When things go well, or we encounter someone who gives us a boost by praising us, our self-image improves. When things go poorly, or when we encounter criticism, our self-image suffers.

You need not be the passive victim of people and events. You have free will. You can control your subconscious self-image. You do it the same way Snead did it in his years of greatness. When you think about golf, you think about your good shots. Think about how you want to play or don't think about playing. Think about putting well, about balls falling into the hole—or don't think about putting. You fall in love with your own talent. You forget your mistakes. You see yourself doing great things. You surround yourself with people who support you.

The process requires honesty. It would be easier if there was a computer somewhere storing all the thoughts you have about yourself each day and creating a printout at the end of the day, with helpful thoughts in black and destructive thoughts in red.

You could look at the printout and know how you'd done that day. If the black ink dominated over the red ink, you'd be fine. But there is no such computer. You have to do this for yourself.

You can monitor your thoughts. Many people find that it helps to keep a little notebook in which they write down everything that comes into their minds, in this case about golf. The mere act of doing this can create a self-awareness that wasn't there before. Thoughts on paper may be easier to assess and weigh than thoughts that flit fitfully through your mind. When it's written down, it's harder to ignore a destructive thought.

Your subconscious never ignores a destructive thought. It's always listening. You don't have to achieve perfection in the thoughts you feed it. Everyone is human and everyone suffers occasional doubts and worries. But you must make sure that helpful thoughts dominate.

# THOUGHTS TO PLAY BY

Your self-image is called that because you create it yourself, with the thoughts you have about yourself and your golf game.

Your subconscious houses your image of yourself.

The subconscious is neither discerning nor selective.

At any given moment, your self-image as a golfer is like a running total of all the thoughts you have about yourself and your game.

Recent thoughts have more impact than older thoughts.

The subconscious will try to accommodate the conscious mind and give it what it thinks the conscious mind wants.

Your subconscious is always listening, so make sure helpful thoughts dominate.

If your self-image is poor, work on it as you would your physical fitness, seeking steady, gradual improvement.

## THREE

# GOALS AND DREAMS

O   O   O

*Achievement, I have heard it said, is largely the*
*product of steadily raising one's levels of aspiration*
*and expectation.*
—*Jack Nicklaus*

Tom Kite pointed out something important in an early discussion we had about goals. When he was a boy, he said, he never particularly liked goals. He felt they were something that adults and coaches imposed. They didn't belong to him.

Tom was energized by his dreams. They were his own. He dreamed of being a great player, of winning major championships. His dreams motivated him. They kept him going through rough patches. They made him believe that a nearsighted kid who was not even considered the most talented junior at his club (Ben Crenshaw was considered the prodigy in Austin, Texas, in those years) could hope to compete with the best in the world. Which, of course, he did. Today, both he and Ben are in the World Golf Hall of Fame. But it wouldn't have been catastrophic for Tom if his career had not been quite so successful. He understood that spending his days chasing his dreams was the best way to assure he'd have a rich and happy life.

Tom helped me arrive at a distinction in the way I discuss goals with players. When I speak of goals now, I am more often not speaking of a player's ultimate objectives, whether they be the Grand Slam or a single-digit handicap. If a player wants to call these goals, that's fine. But I tend to think of them, as Tom does, as dreams.

There's another sort of goal that I speak of often. It's called a "process goal." So often, success comes from patiently and persistently doing the right things over and over. Process goals are the "to-do lists" of players striving for excellence. The process is what gives you a chance to find out how good you can be.

Here, for instance, is a set of process goals for a round of golf that is a more elaborate version of the list of ten principles I gave you in the introduction. If you follow them, you'll give yourself your best chance to find out how well you can play in that particular round:

- I will trust myself and my swing on every shot. I don't have absolute control of where the ball goes. I do have absolute control of whether I trust myself.

- I will execute my pre-shot routine on every shot.

- I will stay in the present moment. I won't speculate in the middle of the round about what my score will be, or where I'll stand in the tournament. I'll stop worrying about not breaking 90, or 70. I will refrain from critiquing or analyzing the shots I've taken. I will focus on each shot as it comes, and that will be the only shot I'll care about. When it's over, I'll see how I did.

- I will refuse to allow anything that happens on the golf course today to bother me or upset me. I will accept bad breaks and mistakes, and be tough in adversity. I am going to be in a good mood and a great state of mind for the entire round today. I'll enjoy playing.

- I will trust my instincts and be decisive and committed.

- I will get looser, freer, and more confident as the round goes on, resisting the urge to get tighter, more careful, and doubtful.

- I will love my wedge and my putter today.

- I will let the ball go to my target on every shot.

- I will maintain a constant, ideal level of intensity on every shot.

- I will play to play great.

These are short-term process goals. There are others that will guide a player through a season or a career. A few of them will be shared by most, if not all, players. Every good player needs to surround himself with people who are helpful and supportive, be they friends, playing partners, spouses, or teachers. He needs to care for and treasure those people.

You might also, for instance, set a goal of doing something every day to give yourself a chance to get a little better. But exactly what you ought to do depends on your game and your circumstances. At some stages in your life, it might be feasible to spend two or three hours practicing every day. At others, the best you can do might be a forty-five-minute indoor session without even getting to a golf course. Your circumstances are unique. So there's no standard set of long-term process goals to list. The process goals for a season and a career need to be custom-tailored. Only you can do it.

Perhaps your process goal will be to practice three times a week and after years of working almost exclusively on long shots, to devote the proper attention to your short game—at least 50 percent of your practice time. Maybe it will be to see your teacher once a month and work on a two-year plan to improve your game. Maybe it will be to work on fitness and flexibility every day. Maybe it will be some combination of these and other possibilities.

In setting process goals, you need to take an honest inventory of your game. Maybe your ball-striking needs improvement. Maybe it's chipping and pitching or bunker play. Maybe it's something in your mental game. You might need to have a better attitude toward putting, or you might need to be better at staying in the present moment. Obviously, no one is perfect in any of these areas. But most players are better in some than in others. Give your inventory the form of a report card. If you're giving yourself B's and A's in most aspects of the game and D's in one, you know how to allot your time and energy. Your inventory will guide you in setting the process goals that are correct for you.

# THOUGHTS TO PLAY BY

**A process goal is an intention to do certain things, often repeatedly, that will lead to the realization of your dreams.**

**Success is a combination of the right process and perseverance.**

**Great golfers learn to be good at waiting, but as they wait, they do the right things.**

FOUR

# HOW MEMORY WORKS

O O O

*The inability to forget is infinitely more devastating
than the inability to remember.*
—*Mark Twain*

Virtually any American born by the mid-1950s can tell you exactly where he or she was on November 22, 1963. That was the day of President John F. Kennedy's assassination. I was a freshman at Mt. St. Joseph Academy in Rutland, Vermont, when the announcement came. I can still remember staring at the loudspeaker in disbelief.

We remember that moment so vividly because of the strong emotions it aroused: shock, grief, fear. Therein lies a lesson about the way the mind works that can help any golfer improve his performance. Memories are much stronger and remain in our minds far longer when we attach strong emotions to events. Conversely, events and thoughts that arouse no emotion are soon forgotten.

The emotions don't have to be negative. Joy works just as

well as grief. If you doubt this, ask any couple if they remember their wedding night. Chances are they remember it far more vividly than they remember last Tuesday. That's because of the strong emotions (joyful emotions, I hope) attached to the event.

Why does this matter to a golfer?

Ideally, a golfer would remember eternally his best shots. When he confronted a difficult tee shot, or a lob from a tight lie, or a slippery putt, he'd recollect all the great shots he'd hit in similar situations in the past. He'd step up to the ball confidently, and this confidence would greatly enhance the chance that he'd hit another great shot.

Unfortunately, too many of us have the opposite tendency. We remember our bad shots, and we forget our good ones.

Our culture pushes us in this direction. From the fourth grade on, when a teacher grades a paper, he usually makes no mark next to a correct answer. He puts a red "X" next to a mistake, calling the child's attention to it. The theory, I suppose, is that we have to remember our mistakes to correct them and avoid repeating them. I'm not sure the theory works all that well in learning the multiplication tables. I know it's disastrous when it comes to golf.

I noticed this when I first started working with Tom Kite. Tom was like a lot of golfers. When he hit a beautiful shot, he felt no emotion. That was, in his mind, merely what he was supposed to do. It was like getting the right answer for "4 x 7 = ?" When he hit a bad shot, though, he got angry. Consequently, he remembered lots of bad shots. He remembered relatively few good ones.

Though this is a common pattern among golfers, it's neither natural nor inevitable. No one is born with Tom's attitude.

Give a small child a golf club and a ball and watch him. He doesn't get angry when he swings and misses, but he beams with delight when he makes contact and gets the ball airborne. The child instinctively understands that hitting a golf ball is not easy. He understands that managing this feat is a cause for celebration and that failing to accomplish it is something to shrug off. It's only later, after years of socialization, that the child learns to do the opposite, to get angry when he misses and shrug it off when he hits a great shot.

Anything that is learned can be unlearned. You can train yourself to have the kind of memory a golfer needs, just as Tom Kite did.

You begin by accepting the fact that golf is a game played by human beings. Therefore, it's a game of mistakes. No one is going to hit every shot correctly in a round of golf. The best players realize this. Ben Hogan used to say that he hit only a few shots perfectly in any round. Jack Nicklaus has said that the key to scoring well is making your misses better.

Because of the way memory works, I like to see players with some of the phlegmatic demeanor Hogan and Nicklaus displayed in their primes. Nicklaus and Hogan might express some frustration with a bad shot. But it's inconceivable that either would lose control enough to cuss or throw a club. They knew better. They knew that it's no coincidence that the best golfers are generally tranquil and poker-faced under duress.

I liked the way Adam Scott reacted when he hit his approach shot into the water on the 72nd hole of the Players Championship in 2004. He showed very little emotion; he blinked once and then started thinking about his next shot. It may have been easier to respond that way because he had a two-shot lead rather than a one-shot lead. He knew he could still win the tournament with a bogey. And he did, taking his drop and lobbing the ball back toward the hole, then making a ten-footer. I suspect he'll have a fairly easy time forgetting the shot that went into the water.

Conversely, I like players to enjoy their good shots. You don't have to be obnoxious about it. There's no need for trash talking or jumping up and down. But when you hit a good shot, take a moment to savor it. Congratulate yourself. Smile. Look around you and notice where you are and what the weather is. Imprint the moment in your memory.

I encourage players to use technology to cement their good memories. I might have them make an audio tape with some of their favorite music in the background. On the tape, they record their memories of their best shots soon after they've happened. Then, at home or in the car, they play the tape. I like them to do it once a day. Tour players have an advantage in that their greatest shots are often on television. I like Tour players to make a highlight video of their finest moments and to watch it regularly.

If machinery is not your style, you don't need it. But you need to sit down every night for fifteen or twenty minutes to review and savor the best shots of your life, or the best shots you've hit recently. When you do, go ahead and enjoy the memories. They should feel very warm and real to you. Remember how the grass smelled and the way the wind ruffled the trees and the sun shone on your face. In your mind, you're putting together the equivalent of a family photo album that shows happy moments on vacation.

It's important to do this because golf is unlike team sports. In team sports, there are lots of people around who are going to pat you on the back when you hit a key basket or make a clutch hit. After the game, they'll be glad to talk to you about it. If you hit a great shot on 18 and you go into the locker room after the round, you find that no one cares and no one wants to talk about it. If you insist, people will think you're a jerk or a braggart. (Oddly enough, if you want to talk about your bad shots after a round, most locker rooms have several people who will be more than happy to listen to your tale of woe and try to top it with their own.)

On the other hand, you want to forget your bad shots almost as soon as they've happened. Have compassion for yourself. Forgive yourself. This will help you forget and move on. Holding on to the memory of a bad shot is a form of punishment. It tends to make you tight and careful when you need to be free and confident. It can compound an error, turning a single bad shot into a skein of them that can ruin a round or a tournament.

It might be worthwhile, on occasion, to chart your rounds to help figure out which parts of your game need improvement most. But no good can come of brooding. There's a belief in our culture that a good athlete ought to be downcast and miserable after a poor performance. He ought to look gloomy and act gloomy. He ought to go to bed without supper and make sure everyone around him knows he's unhappy, knows he's not satisfied. It's a mistaken belief. If you make a bad shot or have a bad round, consider quickly whether there's something you can learn from it that will make your next performance better. After that, forget it.

## THOUGHTS TO REMEMBER BY

Memories are much stronger and remain in our minds far longer when we attach strong emotions to events.

Enjoying your good shots and not responding to your bad ones is infinitely preferable to having no response to your good shots and getting upset at your bad ones.

Keep a notebook or a video log of your great shots.

When you mis-hit a ball, have compassion for yourself. Forgive yourself. This will help you forget your bad shots.

Holding on to the memory of a bad shot is a form of punishment. It tends to make you tight and careful when you need to be free and confident. It can compound an error, turning a single bad shot into a skein of them that can ruin a round or a tournament.

# FIVE

# CONFIDENCE

O   O   O

*Without confidence, a golfer is little more*
*than a hacker.*
—Bobby Jones

If you need a definition of confidence, try this: A confident golfer thinks about what he wants to happen on the course. A golfer who lacks confidence thinks about the things he doesn't want to happen. That's all confidence is. It's not arrogance. It's not experience. It's simply thinking about the things you want to happen on the golf course.

Given two players of equal skills, the more confident one will win nearly all the time. I don't know exactly why that's the case. I only know that our bodies react to the degree of confidence we've nurtured in our conscious and subconscious minds. Play a shot confidently, and the body performs at its graceful best. Play a shot while doubting your ability to pull it off, and the body more often than not loses its rhythm, grace, and timing. Confident golfers play like athletes. They walk onto the course as if they were going to a party filled with people who like and admire them. Golfers who lack confidence step onto the course the way a serious, uptight nerd would walk into that same party.

At the level of a given shot, confidence is no more than the ability to focus the mind and think only about the ball going to the target. You have to see it going there if you've got a graphic imagination. You have to believe it's going there if your imagination is more abstract. It sounds simple, and to a degree it is. But there's a difference between simple and easy. If it were easy, I'd be out of business. Golfers find all sorts of ways to think about the ball not going to the target.

It's an odd thing. Nearly all the players I work with have already mastered the fundamentals. But they're not always confident golfers. Some of them putt more fearfully and carefully on the 72nd green than they do on the first green. They let it go on the first tee and try to steer it on the 18th tee.

The same could be said for millions of amateurs who play in the 70s, 80s, and 90s. They've learned the fundamentals. And yet every year, they finish the season a little less confident than they were before it started. Every round, they play the 18th hole less confidently than they played the first.

Why should this be so? Logically, it makes no sense. Take the case of the tournament player on the 72nd green. He's had four days to get used to the speed and the grain, if there is any. He's had four days of seeing how the ball breaks on this particular course and three days' experience with this particular green. Why shouldn't he be more confident addressing a putt on the final green than he was on the first green? You should be more confident at the end of a round than at the beginning.

You should be more confident at the end of a season than you were at the beginning. If you're not, there's something wrong with the way you're choosing which thoughts you'll entertain.

Some players have a tendency to let golf beat up their psyches. During the course of any four-round tournament, any season, any career, the odds are that you're going to miss some fairways. You're going to miss some makeable putts. That's the nature of the game. The question is, do you choose to remember those misses? Or do you choose to remember the far more frequent good drives, good approaches, and good putts?

In golf, it should be easier to maintain confidence than it is in most other sports. The baseball batter is excellent if he gets a hit one-third of the time. The best football quarterback is going to miss his receivers nearly half the time. Yet .300 hitters and 60 percent passers generally exude confidence.

A competent golfer is like a .900 hitter. He's going to hit the fairway most of the time. He's going to sink his three-foot putts most of the time. He's only being realistic if he thinks confidently when he attempts to hit those shots. So if you don't feel more confident with each passing year of your golf career, if you don't putt more confidently at the end of a round than you do at the beginning, it's a sign that something is amiss with your thinking.

If, instead of remembering those successful shots, you're remembering the misses, your confidence is going to suffer. If your confidence suffers, your performance will suffer.

If that's your problem, you have to go back to what you know about memory and the subconscious. You have to begin allowing yourself to feel joy over your good shots, because that's how you'll cement them in your memory. You have to will yourself to be phlegmatic in the wake of bad shots, because this will help you forget them faster. If need be, you've got to start keeping notes or reviewing videotape that will remind you of your best shots. I recall talking with Fred Couples one night just before he won the 1992 Masters. Fred was not a client, but he asked me what I thought of one aspect of his pre-shot routine. He said that before he hit any shot, he thought about the best shot he'd ever hit with that club in his hands. I was not surprised when he put on the green jacket a few days later. That sort of thinking leads to confidence.

I sometimes speak with players who complain that, "If I had Tiger's record, sure, I'd be confident." It's true that the easiest way to build confidence is to win early and win often, as Tiger did from the time he was a small boy. That was one of the smartest of the many smart things his parents did in raising him. They made certain that he played most of his golf at a level where he could win. Only when he was dominant at one level did they let him move on to the next one.

At his best, Tiger radiated confidence. He felt that if he played his best golf, he was going to win, period. If he played something less than his best, he felt there might be a few guys who could beat him, but not many. And they'd have to be in their best form. In those days, a lot of players looked for Tiger's name on the scoreboard. Tiger didn't look for anyone else's.

But I much more admire those players who, despite not having an early record of success like Tiger's, have managed to become winners at whatever level. I admire Phil Mickelson, who failed in the majors for more than a dozen years yet managed to find the confidence to play a superb back nine in the final round of the 2004 Masters—and win. I admire players like

Tom Lehman and Fred Funk, who struggled to make a living playing golf in their twenties, who at various times went broke and considered other careers, but who persevered and maintained a belief in themselves. They are far better role models than Tiger for most of us. They show how it's possible to develop confidence even without early success. They show that confidence doesn't necessarily come from a full trophy cabinet. Confidence comes from within.

## THOUGHTS TO PLAY BY

Confidence is knowing that if you play the golf you're capable of, you will win or have a chance to win.

Confidence is being more comfortable as your score gets lower and you get in a position to win.

Confidence is feeling like *a* winner even if you're not *the* winner.

You should be more confident at the end of a round than at the beginning.

If you don't grow in confidence with every year you play golf, your thinking needs adjustment.

Thinking confidently about your game should be no different than thinking honestly about your game.

A confident player thinks about what he wants to happen on the course. A player who lacks confidence thinks about what he doesn't want to happen.

Given two players of equal skills, the more confident one will win nearly all the time.

Confidence about a shot is no more than thinking only about the ball going to the target.

Confidence doesn't come from a full trophy cabinet. Confidence comes from within.

# SIX

# STAYING IN THE PRESENT

○ ○ ○

*We just do our best on every possession and*
*assume we will win, but sometimes we simply*
*run out of time.*
—John Wooden

Of all the concepts I teach, staying in the present is perhaps the simplest. Yet it's one of the most difficult to practice.

Superficially, what could be easier? We are always in the present moment. Our being there defines it as the present. But the mind is not fettered by the same constraints as the body. In an instant, the mind can flit from the present to the past and from the past to the future.

Golf presents continuous opportunities to let the mind wander. If you are, say, a hockey goalie, and the puck is in your end, you're constrained to stay in the present, because the puck can come at you at any moment. But long pauses have been built into golf. We walk between shots. We wait for playing partners to hit the ball. In tournaments, we wait overnight from one round to the next. That's a lot of idle time, and the mind is always tempted to fill that time with thoughts of the past and the future.

I have clients who tell me that staying in the present is no problem for them. But then they say something like, "I came to the 16th, and I'm thinking, this is a birdie hole . . ."

I have to stop them and point out the implication of what they've just said. If you step onto the tee thinking, "this is a birdie hole," you're already thinking two or three shots ahead of the present moment. A player who is truly in the present steps onto the tee and thinks only of how he wants to hit his tee shot. He doesn't think about what he ought to or will make on the hole. He thinks about his tee shot. He hits it. He accepts it. He finds it. He thinks about his next shot. He repeats the process till the ball is in the hole or until he's run out of holes.

If your mind is truly in the present, you don't evaluate how you're playing, because that would mean you're thinking about the past. You don't judge or critique for the same reason.

Nor do you keep a running tally of your score, thinking as you do that if you can par in you'll break 70, or 80, or whatever. That would mean thinking about both the past (the score is, after all, the sum of the strokes you've made in the past) and the future (the total you'll have at the end of the round).

I talked recently with a young client who's playing mini-tour events, trying to get himself ready for the PGA Tour's qualifying school. He said that he'd been playing very well on the mini-tour, winning a couple of events. He felt confident. He entered the Monday qualifier for a PGA Tour event in Atlanta. He told his wife he was playing so well he thought he might win the whole tournament.

Instead, he said he played "tight and scared" and didn't even make the field. He couldn't understand what had happened to the confident golf he'd been playing on the mini-tour.

I knew immediately what had happened. On the mini-tour, the client was not particularly concerned about the results. He focused on his pre-shot routine, on making each shot a quality shot. He was into the process we'd talked about, the process of hitting his best golf shots.

When he stepped off the mini-tour, he forgot about that. He started thinking about the future, as evidenced by the fact that he told his wife he thought he might win the whole tournament. Consequently, with his mind not in the present, he played "tight and scared"—and badly.

If your mind is truly in the present, you don't play "tight and scared." You don't get overly excited or discouraged on the golf course. Excitement would suggest that you're thinking about the outcome of the round. Discouragement would suggest that you're both mired in the past mistakes you've made and worried about the final result. You don't pay attention to how others in the field are playing, and if you happen to see a scoreboard, it means almost nothing to you. Thinking about how others are playing is another form of thinking about the future, because the only reason you could care about how they're playing is a premature interest in how the tournament will end—the result.

The golfer who stays in the present just keeps playing the shot at hand until he runs out of holes. Then he adds it up.

John Wooden used to coach his UCLA basketball teams to play in the present. Wooden's philosophy was to play the best possible basketball on each possession. Only when time expired did he want his Bruins to be very conscious of the score. Sometimes, he said, time ran out on his teams. But more often than not, playing each possession with their minds in the present moment worked very well. Wooden's teams won ten national championships.

Why is staying in the present so important?

It's because golf requires a narrow focus on one thing: where you want the ball to go. Anything that detracts from that focus damages your ability to play. Golf history is littered with stories of players who were well on their way to winning major championships until they made the fatal mistake of thinking, while there were still holes left to play, about whether they should take their hats off when they received the trophy.

Maybe the most famous example is Arnold Palmer in the 1961 Masters. Palmer had a one-stroke lead when he came to the 72nd hole, and he hit a fine drive. He seemed certain to become the first player to win back-to-back Masters. As he walked toward his ball, an old friend in the gallery beckoned him over. "Nice going, boy," the friend said. "You won it."

Palmer made a critical mistake. He accepted the friend's congratulations and shook his hand. In doing so, "I completely destroyed my concentration," he acknowledged later.

With his mind no longer in the present moment, Palmer hit his approach into a bunker, hit a poor bunker shot and wound up making six, handing the tournament to Gary Player.

It was a strong, bitter lesson, and yet staying in the present was not something Palmer, despite being one of the great golfers of all time, completely mastered. Five years later, with a seven-stroke lead in the final round of the U.S. Open, he started thinking about breaking the tournament scoring record instead of staying in the present and playing one shot at a time. Not coincidentally, he shot 39 for the final nine holes and was overtaken by Billy Casper.

As Palmer's experience shows, staying in the present isn't easy. In fact, I don't think I've ever met a player who's mastered it. It's one of the most difficult things a golfer has to do, and it's something that competitive players have to work on constantly, striving just to be very good at it.

It's much easier to stay lost in the present if you have peace of mind. If you knew that you were going to win a tournament, or that you'd have a great year, or that your career would see the fulfillment of all your dreams, you'd have far less incentive to worry about the future or critique the past. You need to try to play as if you knew those things.

You want to stay in the present until there are no more holes to play and then worry about the result. Of course, you'd rather have the final tally show you've won. If you stay in the present, it will do that more often.

## THOUGHTS TO PLAY BY

Stay in the present. The only shot you think about is the one at hand.

During a round, there is no evaluating. There is no judging. There is no anticipating the result. There is only trust and acceptance.

Anything that detracts from a narrow focus on the shot at hand diminishes your chances of playing your best golf.

It's natural to stay in the present if you have complete peace of mind.

When you run out of holes, and only when you've run out of holes, add it up and see how you've done.

# SEVEN

# YOUR TARGET

O   O   O

*I'm not going to get the ball close. I'm going
to sink it.*
—Tom Watson, before chipping in on the 71st
hole, 1982 U.S. Open

Imagine a man lost in a desert. He's been without water for
days. He's hot, he's thirsty, he's staggering. Suddenly, on the
horizon, he sees palm trees and vegetation—an oasis. He understands that the oasis contains the water that can save his
life. He turns toward it. His eyes lock onto those palm trees on
the horizon. Getting there consumes his entire consciousness.
He walks steadily toward it. He pays no attention to rocks or
dunes or other obstacles. He thinks only of the oasis.

That's the way a golfer should feel about his target.

When a player is properly into his target, it's as if there were
a laser beam linking his mind and the spot where he wants the
ball to go. Nothing else exists for him. He's very single-minded.

Hazards like woods and water don't distract him. Once he's picked his target, he thinks only of the ball going there.

I recall talking to Davis Love III after he won the 2003 Players Championship. One of the many great shots Davis hit that day was a 6-iron out of the trees to the 16th green, where he putted in for an eagle. If you've played that course or seen it on television, you know that the 16th green perches on the edge of a lake. It's protected on the dry side by mounds, rough, bunkers, and a tree. On the day of the final round, the hole was cut very close to the lake, and Davis's shot ended up very close to the hole. I asked him whether he had aimed for the middle of the green and pushed the shot.

"Doc, I was so there and so into the target I could see nothing but the flag, I promise you. I hit that exactly where I was looking," Davis said.

That's not to say that all golfers should take dead aim from long range at a pin perched on the edge of a pond. It depends on the player's skill and the club he has in his hand. When you have a wedge or a chipping club in your hand, the target will almost certainly be the hole. But whether you're aiming at the flag or a tree behind the middle of the green, your attention to your target should be intense and single-minded.

That kind of focus on a target greatly improves the prospect that the ball will, indeed, go to it. The more you're consumed with your target, the more your instincts and subconscious will help you find it. It's as if you have an automatic guidance system, like a heat-seeking missile's. Not all missiles hit their targets and you won't always hit yours. But if you're into the target, the ball will go there more often. You're far less likely to mis-hit a shot, and your misses will be more playable. I don't know why the human organism works this way. I only know that it does.

You want the smallest possible target you can see without squinting. On short putts, this might be a single blade of grass overhanging the edge of the hole. On longer putts, it might be a portion of the hole. It could be a point on the green outside the hole if you're the sort who prefers to putt to a point, say, two balls outside the right edge on a putt that breaks gently from right to left. On chips, it can be either the hole itself or a spot where you want the chip to land before it rolls to the hole. On long shots, the target could be the flag, a tree branch, a steeple, or anything else you can see easily and distinctly.

There's a wide individual variation in the way players perceive targets. Some people tell me they envision a dotted line running from their ball to the hole. Some people see a railroad track, a chute, or a path burned into the green. I've had players tell me they see a trajectory rather than a target. Others see the ball popping out of the hole and running backward to their clubs. That's all fine. The only necessity is that what you see is relevant to where you want the ball to go.

Look at the target with soft eyes. By that, I mean that I don't want your body to get rigid because you're staring too intensely at the target. Caress it with your sight.

Some players, like Nick Price, have the gift of being able to see the target in their mind's eye after they've turned their eyes back to the ball. It's as if they had a third eye in the side of their head, an eye that remains focused on the target even after they start their swing. But while this can be helpful, it isn't necessary to be so visual. As long as you pick a target and think only of sending the ball to that target, you're fine. Your brain remembers where the target is just as it remembers where the chest of drawers is in a dark hotel room. If you get up groggy in the middle of the night in a strange room, you pick your way around the obstacles in your path even though you only saw them once. Somewhere in your mind, the memory lingers. Target orientation is like that.

When you've picked a target, let the ball go to the target. Don't try to guide the ball or steer it. Swing freely and confidently. The trick is to be focused on the target, but at the same time swing as freely as if you needed only to hit a ball off a beach and into the ocean.

# THOUGHTS TO AIM BY

Good golfers have a laser-like focus on their targets.

The more your mind is consumed with the target, the more
your instincts and subconscious will help you.

Some players "see" the target in their mind's eye after they
return their gaze to the ball, but this isn't necessary.

Pick out the smallest possible target you can easily see.

Players envision targets in different ways. Some see a point,
some see a path, some see a trajectory. The only requirement
is that what you see is relevant to where you want the
ball to go.

Look at the target with "soft eyes."

Swing freely and let the ball go to the target. There's no
guiding. There's no steering.

# EIGHT

# ANGER AND ACCEPTANCE

O   O   O

*It took a while to learn it, but eventually I got
it into my head to never get beyond being
sensibly irritated.*
—Sam Snead

When I see a golfer showing anger or irritation over a mis-hit shot, I know one thing immediately. The player is not staying in the present. His mind is in the past, focused on a shot that's already been played—that's gone.

Every shot you make on a golf course creates a new hole. The object of the game is to get the ball from the point where it rests into the hole you're playing in the fewest strokes possible. It doesn't matter how the ball got to the spot where it's resting.

I view anger and frustration as impediments to playing that new game. For starters, if you're angry, you're not focused on the only shot that matters, your next one. You're focused on the last shot. On top of that, anger introduces tension into the body. Tension damages rhythm and grace. It hinders your effort to get your mind and body into the state where you play your best golf.

There's a bit of destructive self-indulgence in permitting yourself to be angry. And you do permit it. Anger is a choice. It's not caused by anyone else. Anger is the way you choose to respond to an irritating event.

I've met players who tell me that anger helps them focus and concentrate. They tell me that once they get angry, it's as if they have tunnel vision, that all they see is the golf course and the shot they need to hit. That's possible. Golf gives us time between shots, and it's certainly within the realm of human capability to hit a bad shot, get angry, and then focus on the task at hand while you're moving toward your next shot. But why would you choose to engage in something that distracts you?

I have had players tell me that while they might get angry on a Sunday morning when they're out of contention, they would never permit themselves to do so if they were in the hunt on Sunday afternoon. They may think that. But we are all prone to habit, and if you get in the habit of being angry, you may not be able to control when the habit emerges.

Indulging your anger is a risky way to play golf. (It can also be quite obnoxious to the people playing with you.) I've seen too many players get angry, then lose themselves in self-pity as the anger fades. I've seen others let their anger overwhelm them. They lose their judgment about strategy and shot selection. They compound their initial error with more errors, until their round and their tournament are ruined. Other players let anger lead them to start criticizing themselves and their swings. That's another way to be distracted from the task at hand.

I much prefer my clients to practice a virtue that's not very fashionable at the moment. I want them to accept whatever happens to a shot and move on. Most people have been brought up in a culture that views acceptance as a weakness rather than a strength. It's viewed as giving in, giving up, not caring. It's definitely not very macho. We live in a society that talks proudly about "zero defects" and "zero tolerance." To an ambitious golfer, the natural tendency becomes refusal to accept mistakes. But in golf, because humans are flawed and the game is so difficult, mistakes are going to happen. Accepting them is not a weakness. It's a very important part of getting stronger and mentally tougher, a part of resilience, of being able to hang in there during a round, recover from errors and finish with a good score.

Padraig Harrington tells me that he's performed better since he made acceptance part of his pre-shot routine. As he prepares to hit a shot, Padraig reminds himself that whatever happens to it, he will accept it and go from there. This allows him to focus narrowly on his target and swing freely.

Acceptance, of course, is to be practiced on the course, during a round of golf. After it's over, it's fine to make a quick assessment of where you made your mistakes. It's fine to lay out a plan to improve your weaknesses. I'm not advocating accepting mediocrity and poor results. I'm advocating just the opposite. Acceptance doesn't preclude thorough preparation and practice to improve your skills.

Acceptance is tightly linked to the patience that is required of all great golfers. If you play golf, you have to accept and understand from the outset that weird things are going to happen to your golf ball. If you're thinking right, you accept that everything might not go your way. The more you accept, the easier it is to keep playing and the more quickly something good will happen.

## THOUGHTS TO KEEP COOL BY

Every shot you make creates a new hole.

The player who is angry is not staying in the present. He's focused on the past.

Anger is always a choice and is never caused by someone else or something else.

Displays of anger during a round indicate that something has become more important than the shot at hand.

Anger introduces tension into the body.

Most experienced competitors view displays of anger as signs of immaturity or loss of control.

Accept whatever happens to a shot and move on.

# NINE

# PLANNING FOR SUCCESS

O   O   O

*Your performance has a way of living up to
your expectations.*
—*Arnold Palmer*

You may think that a good round of golf starts on the first tee.
It doesn't. A good round of golf starts well before the player
takes his first swing. It starts with his game plan.

A golfer's game plan incorporates a strategy for playing every
hole. But it's more than that. A complete game plan anticipates
all the contingencies that can arise in a round of golf. It prepares
the golfer to cope with those contingencies. No matter what
happens on the course, a player with a good game plan has the
sense that he's foreseen the possibility. He already knows the
most sensible response because he's thought that through in advance. He suffers no uncertainty, no doubt. He merely executes
his plan. Playing in this state of mind, he produces better shots,
because his mind is clear.

Hole-by-hole strategy is actually the easiest part of the game plan to prepare. I never try to prescribe strategy for a player. It depends on so many things that only the player can know. Take, for an example, the 18th hole at the TPC Sawgrass, the site each year of the Players Championship. It's a long par four, shaped like a banana curving left, with a lake running down the left side. Some players hit their driver off the tee. Some hit a three-wood. Some hit an iron. The right choice will be dictated by the strengths of the player's game. If he hits a driver, is he confident he can bend it right-to-left enough to stay in the fairway but not so much as to hit the water? Or should he hit a three-wood, knowing that he turns that club over more easily, or that even if he hits it straight, he's not going to run out of fairway? The correct answer varies with the player and perhaps varies from week to week, or day to day. It varies with the wind. It varies with individual skills. Some players feel more confident about hitting a gentle draw with their drivers than others. Some will feel confident about their drivers one week and not another week. All I tell a player about a hole like No. 18 at Sawgrass is that he needs to plan for every situation that might prevail when he steps onto the tee.

On most golf courses, there are going to be a couple of holes that will make at least some players uncomfortable hitting their drivers. If you're a long hitter on a tight course with a lot of doglegs, there may be more than a few such holes. A smart game plan will call for another club on those tees. But I never try to tell a player which tees. The only things I insist on is that their game plans reflect an honest assessment of the strengths of their games and that whatever club they plan to use is a club they can use under pressure with absolute trust.

There's a misperception that thinking confidently means thinking recklessly, that a confident golfer shoots at every pin. He doesn't. A golfer both smart and confident, after honestly assessing his own strengths, takes aim at the pin in some situations and stays away from it in others. Let's suppose there's a long par four with a green that tilts back to front. There's a rear tier to this green, and immediately beyond it are bunkers and thick rough. On top of that, the tournament committee has set the course up with hard greens. A smart game plan takes account of the fact that, given the length of the hole, the approach to the green will almost certainly be made with a mid-to-long iron. If a player were to try to land such a club on the back tier, attacking the pin, it would most likely bounce over the green, leaving a tough recovery from a difficult lie toward a tight pin cut in a green that slopes away from the player. A smart game plan recognizes that under most circumstances, it's best not to shoot at sucker pins. A smart game plan will dictate that the player on our example hole aims for the center of the green in most situations, since he's got a mid-iron or longer club in his hands. (The calculation changes, obviously, if the club is a short iron or a wedge.) He takes his chances with a longer birdie putt.

The decision that you hear about most on golf telecasts— whether to try to reach a par five green in two shots—is actually one of the more formulaic in a game plan. With most good players it becomes an automatic process. Hit the tee shot a certain distance, go for it. Hit it less than the threshold distance, lay up. There can be complicating factors such as the nature of the hazards around a green. If there's an out-of-bounds or water penalty for an errant shot, it might change the threshold distance. If a stiff wind is in the player's face, his plan might call for him to hit a three-wood, a 4-iron and a pitching wedge and rely on his putter for a birdie. If the wind's at his back, he might hit a driver and then a three-wood and try to reach the green.

The wind is one of the many contingencies a player must plan for. If you're a Scottish player whose home course is a seaside links, it's not really a contingency. You can just assume that the wind will be blowing. But for many American players, wind is not a regular factor. When it blows, they must be prepared. Will they move the ball back in their stance and try to hit lower shots? Do they feel confident enough of their ability to work the ball in both directions that they can plan to curve the ball against a quartering wind? Or will they just plan to hit their normal shots and make whatever allowance for the wind that seems appropriate at the time? Again, the right answer will depend on an individual's strengths.

Rain is another environmental factor that can throw players off if they're not prepared for it. Anticipating rain, obviously, you'll want to give yourself peace of mind by knowing that your rain gear, from extra gloves and towels to waterproof pants, is set to go. The major game plan adjustment that will probably be required of you is extra patience. You have to make up your mind in advance that if it rains, nothing will bother you. You won't care if the pace of play slows down. You'll even take pleasure in the fact that a lot of your competition will let the rain affect their games. If there's a three-hour rain delay that stops you in the middle of a string of birdies, you'll anticipate that, as well. You'll stay relaxed and focused and you won't let it frustrate you.

You must also plan for scoring and competitive contingencies. Suppose that you start off your round hitting the ball beautifully and make several birdies on the opening holes. Do you try to figure out what's suddenly gone right with your swing? Or do you say to yourself, "Okay, I'm hot today and I'm going to ride it to the lowest score I can possibly make"?

Suppose, on the other hand, you start off with five straight bogeys and you can't find the clubhead. It happens. I don't want anyone dwelling on this possibility, visualizing each gory detail. But I do want players to think about the positive way they'd respond to this contingency, how they'd be calm and steady, how they'd stick with their game plans and routines, and how they'd be proud to get back to one or two over par and stay in the tournament, proud of how they held themselves together.

If you're playing tournament golf, you might plan for a few more contingencies, but only rarely should a player's position in a tournament affect his game plan and his strategy for a particular hole. That strategy, after all, was designed to give the player his lowest possible score. Only rare circumstances could justify changing it.

But, let's suppose that the 18th hole of the course you're playing is a very penal one, with water on one side and out-of-bounds on the other. Let's suppose you reach the tee in the final round with a three-stroke lead. Do you change your game plan to make sure you make no worse than a double-bogey?

This, of course, is roughly the situation that faced Jean Van de Velde in the 1999 British Open. I'm not one of those who think Van de Velde necessarily made a mistake in trying to play the final hole of that event as he did—hitting driver off the tee and then going for the green with a long iron. He got a freakish bad break when his ball hit the railing of the grandstand and caromed into knee-high rough near the burn. A few inches either way and he'd have hit the grandstand, gotten a free drop, and made no worse than five. I'm certainly not of the opinion that the smart thing to do would have been to hit three 9-irons to the green. You don't get to the point of leading a major championship by three strokes because you're swinging badly. Playing the hole that cautiously might have done such damage to his concentration and confidence that he'd hit the ball in the water anyway.

The only thing I would have asked Van de Velde was whether he had a plan that covered the contingency of coming to the 72nd hole with a substantial lead. If he didn't, that was a mistake. You don't want to stand on the tee in such a situation and think, "What do I do now?" You want to stand there and think, "Everything is going according to plan."

# THOUGHTS TO PLAN BY

Thorough preparation breeds confidence.

A complete game plan anticipates all the contingencies that can arise in a round of golf.

The right strategy for a given hole is dictated first by the strengths of a player's game.

There is a difference between planning confidently and planning recklessly.

Slow play, wind, and rain are contingencies you must plan for.

You must plan for a great start or a poor start, for leading the tournament or coming from behind.

# TEN

# TRUST

O   O   O

*You must develop enough confidence in your swing
so you can trust it completely.*
—Byron Nelson

Trust is a must.

When we hit a golf ball in competition, we want as much as possible to govern our bodies with our subconscious mind. That's because, in sports, the human organism works most effectively when the conscious mind is shut off. Call it instinct, or intuition, or the right side of the brain if you're more comfortable with those concepts than you are with the notion of the subconscious. Whatever you call it, you want it in control when you play golf. You want to swing thinking only of your target.

To go unconscious, to play instinctively and intuitively, you must trust your swing. You must believe that it will work. That's easy to preach. It's harder to practice. Many of us are trained to be self-critical, to analyze our mistakes and our flaws. That might be helpful in some academic endeavors, but it's fatal to a golfer when he's on the golf course, competing, trying to score.

I'm not saying that there's no place and no time in golf for conscious thought, self-criticism, and analysis. I am saying that the place is the practice range and the time is well before competition. Then, perhaps with the help of a teacher, you can pick apart the position of your club at the top of the backswing, or the way your hands rotate through impact, or whatever else might be wrong with your mechanics. You can think consciously about trying to make those mechanics better.

If you let yourself do that on the golf course, bad things are going to happen. You'll lose your focus on the target. You'll lose your natural grace, timing and rhythm. Trying to control your swing or stroke with the conscious mind, you'll tend to get awkward and stiff.

To explain this, I've sometimes used the analogy of the balance beam. Lay it on the floor and people can walk from one end to the other with no problems. They trust their ability to walk a straight line. But put the beam fifteen feet in the air and ask people to walk it. They start being very careful about where they place their feet. They forget to trust the fact that they know how to walk a straight line. They start thinking about how they're going to place one foot in front of the other. If you actually carried out this experiment, you'd find that many more people would fall from the beam at fifteen feet than would fall from the beam on the floor. The difference would be lack of trust, and the same factor can affect a golf swing.

Still, some players have difficulty bringing themselves to trust. They feel guilty about it, as if swinging with trust wasn't trying hard enough. Trying hard and being careful and "really working at it" are very dear to them. They feel like they're slacking off if they simply go unconscious and trust their swings. "When I just see it [the target] and do it [the swing] I feel like you've taken away all the stuff that I love doing," one player said to me.

I tell such players the idea isn't to try your hardest—it's to try your best. The idea isn't to do what you've always done—unless you want to get results like you've always gotten.

I remind my professional clients that they already know how to hit the shot. I've seen pros who can stand around a practice green all day and hit perfect chip after perfect chip get tight and careful when they have to hit a similar chip in competition. It's a constant struggle for them to trust their skills. But they have to do it.

I work with other players who can trust as long as they're hitting the ball well. As soon as they mis-hit a ball, their trust evaporates. They try to fix their swing, and they start thinking mechanically. There's a certain logic to this. If your swing produces a bad shot, it's obviously flawed. Why should you trust a flawed swing?

The answer is that everyone has a flawed swing, at least occasionally, and thinking mechanically is not going to make it better. It's going to make it worse. Very few players know their own mechanics well enough to make an accurate diagnosis of what went wrong in a golf swing, particularly if it occurs on the course. For one thing, most of the swing occurs behind their heads, out of their field of vision. For another, it happens so quickly that sometimes only slow-motion videotape can pinpoint the cause for a bad shot. And for a third, people perceive their movements inaccurately. If you ask a player to make an adjustment of, say, two inches in his swing plane, it initially feels like two feet.

More important, thinking about and trying to fix mechanics will usually produce a worse result than trusting in your flawed swing. The correct response to a bad shot is to forget about it. On the next shot, execute your pre-shot routine. Swing unconsciously. Trust it. If you feel the need to fix your mechanics, wait till after the round and go to the range to do it.

If you find yourself in a position where you can't trust your swing on the shot you're planning, the answer is not to go ahead and hit the shot anyway. The answer is to plan another shot. If you're standing on the tee with driver in your hands and a creek on the left and the white stakes on the right are intimidating you, don't try to steer the drive between the hazards. If you can't trust your driver in such circumstances, take another club—a fairway wood or an iron. I don't care if you have to drop down to a 5-iron to be able to trust your swing. You're better off hitting the 5-iron unconsciously and accepting the reduced yardage than you are hitting the driver in doubt.

Around the greens, the same principle applies. There may be delicate shots from tight lies that cause a player to lose trust. In such cases, the wise course is to switch plans and try to hit a shot you can trust. Maybe instead of a high lob off a tight lie over a bunker, you hit more of a chip shot. Maybe you putt from off the green instead of chipping. Maybe you use a three-wood or four-wood from the collar and just roll the ball to the hole. There's nothing wrong with any of those options. I've seen great players resort to them. They are great players because they know that the "correct" shot, hit in doubt, is going to be worse than a shot hit with trust. They just want to find a way to get the ball in the hole, unconsciously.

Take the conscious, doubting, self-critical, analytical, and careful side of your mind and stick it in your locker before you play. Tape over the air holes. Make sure it can't get out.

Trusting your swing is really about trusting yourself. Players sometimes ask me for "something I can trust" before they go out on the course for a competitive round. I always tell them, "Okay, I'll give you something you can trust. It's you."

## THOUGHTS TO TRUST BY

The human organism performs best in athletics when the
conscious mind is turned off.

In competition, you must trust your swing. There is no
justification for failing to trust.

If you don't feel you can trust your swing on a given shot,
plan a different shot with a different club or a different line.

In competition, failing to trust a flawed swing will make it
worse, not better.

If you don't trust yourself, you'll only trust your swing when
it's working perfectly.

Think about your swing mechanics only on the practice range.

# ELEVEN

# BUTTERFLIES

O　O　O

*I try to make pressure and tension work for me. I
want the adrenalin to be flowing.*
—Hale Irwin

I sometimes get a call from a player who, for the first time, has
to spend Saturday night sitting on the lead in a tournament. Or,
maybe it's someone who's about to start the Tour's qualifying
school. Maybe it's a college player headed for his first NCAA
championship. It could be an amateur playing for the first time
in his club's championship flight. Whatever the case, what I
usually hear is a variation on this: "Doc, I've got butterflies."

My immediate response is, "Great!"

I say that because I don't think butterflies, or nervous tension, that sense in your stomach that you're in uncharted wa-
ters, are to be feared. I think they're to be welcomed. You don't
get butterflies on Saturday night if you're in 62nd place and the
only thing at stake on Sunday is the few thousand extra dollars

they'd pay you if you shot 66 and moved up to 43rd. You get butterflies when you put yourself in position to realize a dream.

Butterflies, when you think about it, are among Nature's most beautiful creations. When they approach a flower, the flower opens itself up to them. They're integral to the process of pollination.

Like the flower, good golfers welcome the butterflies. They recognize that butterflies are a sign that their hard work is paying off, that they're in the position they've wanted to be in. They recognize that they had to be playing well just to get there. "Pressure makes me more intent about each shot," Nancy Lopez once said. "Pressure on the last few holes makes me play better."

This doesn't mean that good players don't cope with the same physical symptoms of the butterflies that novices feel. They do. Their palms sweat. Their stomachs knot. Their hands tremble. But they welcome those symptoms. They even come to depend on them. Without them, they're a little bored. Toward the end of his career, Jack Nicklaus needed the pressure of being in contention to get interested. When he was, he played well. When he wasn't, he played indifferently.

The only time butterflies become harmful is when we let our fear of them control us. If you panic at the onset of butterflies, you can set off a very strong physical reaction in your body, the fight-or-flight response. It causes a gush of hormones that can turn the butterflies into demons and your body into a trembling mess.

What sometimes happens in this case is that an inexperienced player gets still more panicky. He stops doing the things he knows how to do. He starts worrying about his trembling hands or his dry throat. Consequently, he's not thinking about where he wants the ball to go. He plays badly. Thereafter, when the butterflies re-emerge, he tends to panic again, thinking that they were the cause of his poor play.

Learn to love the butterflies, or at least to handle them. One way some players handle them is to downplay the importance of today's round or tournament and think of all the reasons why it doesn't matter all that much. As Yogi Berra once said to his pitcher in a tight game, "There's a billion Chinese who don't care at all what you do here."

Taking deep, slow breaths can he helpful. Visualizing what you want can be helpful. The calmer and clearer you can keep your mind, the more you can keep it focused on what you want, the more the butterflies will calm down and fly in formation.

Recognize that the physical sensations you feel are caused by adrenalin, which is a natural product of your body, a friend that will help you play better if you keep your mind clear. Remember that fear of the butterflies is in reality fear of your own body.

Be into the target and execute your routine. The fight-or-flight response needn't consume you. In golf, we're not fleeing, and we're not going to hit anybody.

Make the butterflies fly right.

## THOUGHTS TO PLAY BY

**Good golfers cope with the same nervous symptoms everyone else does. But good golfers welcome the butterflies.**

**The only time butterflies become harmful is when we let fear of them control us.**

**Fear of the butterflies is in reality fear of your own body.**

**If you're nervous, so are those playing against you.**

# TWELVE

# YOUR FELLOW GOLFERS

O   O   O

*I learn golf from golfers.*
*—Harvey Penick*

Every time I walk onto the practice range at a professional tournament, I see something rarely, if ever, seen in other sports. I see competitors helping one another. They give swing tips. They give encouragement.

They do this even on the course. Think of Fred Funk and Phil Mickelson exchanging high fives and pats on the back during the final round of the 2004 U.S. Open. They were competitors, but they were also friends. They didn't see a conflict between the two roles.

In team sports, there are rules that prohibit this. Players may on occasion be friends with players on another team, but you'd never see a member of one N.B.A. team coaching a member of the opposition during the pre-game warm-ups. Tennis is an individual sport, but players don't help one another much there, either.

A few years ago, Jim Courier, then one of the top-ranked tennis players in the world, was working with me at my home. I got a call from Brad Faxon, with whom I'd been working for many years. I put Jim on the phone with Brad, and they had a long talk. Afterwards, Courier was amazed.

"He just told me all the most important things he'd learned in ten years of working with you," Courier said. "No one in tennis would ever do that!"

Maybe that's because golfers rarely play directly against one another the way tennis players do. They play against the course and against themselves. Whatever the reason, one of the healthiest things about golf is, or ought to be, the relationships between the competitors.

I like players to think of their fellow competitors as friends rather than enemies. They are, after all, essential to the joy of playing competitive golf. It would be no fun to try to get better if you had no one else's performance against which to measure your own. I like players to have the attitude that their improvement will help their friends get better; their friends' improvement will help them get better. There are enough dollars and trophies to go around.

Most touring pros get this. I find it lacking sometimes in junior golf. Parents, friends and teachers, sadly, will sometimes create bad blood among competitors, because they can't stand the idea of someone beating their child. You hear the occasional, "I hate so-and-so."

I counsel players of all ages that it's a waste of energy to hate a fellow competitor, if for no other reason than you'll probably wind up paired with that person in an important round some day. You won't need the distraction.

Besides, you play golf because of the happiness it brings you. It brings you more happiness if you do it with friends. I'm reminded of Tom Lehman, who played with his friend, Steve Jones, in the final pairing of the 1996 U.S. Open. Both men are deeply religious. And though they were both trying to win a prize Lehman dearly wanted, he had the character on the first tee to share with his friend a Bible verse, telling him that the Lord wanted them both to be courageous and strong. Jones took heart from that verse and, in the end, won the Open by a stroke over Lehman.

But whenever I see Tom Lehman, he strikes me as a very happy man.

## THOUGHTS TO PLAY BY

One of the healthiest things about golf ought to be the relationship between competitors.

If you allow yourself to be irritated by a fellow golfer, it's all but certain you'll be paired with him for the most important round of your life.

Fellow competitors force you to get better, and you in turn force them to get better. Healthy competitors understand this.

Strive to be friends with your fellow competitors. Without them, after all, you would have no one to measure yourself against.

# THIRTEEN

# PRACTICING TO PLAY GREAT

○ ○ ○

*I always practice as I intend to play.*
*—Jack Nicklaus*

One of the most common questions I get from players is a variation of this one: "Doc, I hit the ball really great on the range. But when I get onto the course, I'm a different player. I don't hit the ball nearly as well as I do in practice."

If this sounds like something you'd say, you probably don't suffer from some esoteric psychological problem, like a subconscious desire to fail. It may simply be that you don't practice properly, and you don't know how to take your game from the practice area to the golf course.

The only reason for practice is to get you prepared for the most important shot of your life. Maybe it's the tee shot on No. 18 at Pebble Beach when you're tied for the lead at the U.S. Open and the wind is whipping up whitecaps on Carmel Bay. Maybe it's the first tee shot of your office's annual scramble with your boss watching. Whatever the case, you need to make sure that your practice simulates those conditions as closely as possible.

Golf is one of the few sports where practice typically doesn't occur on the playing field. Baseball players practice on a baseball field. Basketball players practice on the same floor they play their games on. But golfers practice on the range or the putting green, and play on the course.

Among the first things I tell players is that simply raking one ball after another into position and hitting all of them into the vast expanse of a driving range is not going to help them very much in the sort of situation we're talking about. There are no consequences for a poor shot on the range. Psychologically, it's not at all like hitting a shot on a course in competition.

The first thing you must do as you prepare for competition is to make the practice experience as similar as possible to the competitive experience. This means, where possible, practice on the actual course. Hit the ball from the rough and from uneven lies. Drive it between trees and bunkers.

If you're restricted to the range, you'll need to pick out a small, specific target for your shot. You ought to use other indicators on the range—flags and yardage signs—to represent in your mind the edges of the fairway or green you're trying to hit. Make them as narrow as the fairways and greens on the course you'll be playing.

More important, use your full routine on every shot you hit. Imagine a competitive situation and put yourself in it. Then go through the process of checking the wind, pulling a club, taking a practice swing, and lining yourself up. Do it exactly as you would on the golf course. Then hit the shot.

If your shot doesn't come off as planned, accept it, just as you'd have to accept it on the golf course. You might feel an urge to begin immediately trying to fix whatever flaw in your swing you think caused the problem. Especially as competition nears, resist this temptation. You may or may not be able to diagnose correctly what went wrong with your golf swing. But it's certain that trying to fix it will engage your conscious mind in thinking about swing mechanics, and that's not something you should be doing as you compete. You want to be focusing on your target and swinging freely.

Some players on the pro tours like to have their swing teachers on hand to watch them warm up for a competitive round. The idea is that the teacher will be able to fix any flaws that crop up in the final moments of rehearsal. I don't like to see this. If it were up to me, the teacher would either absent himself from the range on the day of competition or limit himself to telling the player how good his swing looks. Even if the teacher does see a flaw and diagnose it correctly, his prescription will probably get the player thinking mechanically.

Of course, it's frequently the player's fault that this happens. Some players, as a competition approaches, tend to panic when they mis-hit a shot. They demand that the teacher tell them what went wrong. If the teacher doesn't know or doesn't want to say, these players will go looking for someone else until they find somebody who will tell them what they did wrong. I have rarely seen this sort of panicked practice lead to good results on the course.

The week before a tournament is not the time to start making a swing change. If the tournament means a lot to you, you need a long-range plan to get ready for it. If you and your teacher decide that this plan should include some swing changes, make them early on. By the week before the tournament, you should be down to making choices about the clubs you'll carry to play a particular course. You should be sharpening your short game, working a bit on any specialty shots you might need for the course, and playing practice rounds. Your time on the range should taper off.

Good players usually have a routine that guides them through the actual competition. It begins with learning their tee times for the first two rounds. Those times determine their schedules for the preceding day. They've learned how much sleep they need to play their best, and they make sure they get it. They've learned what kind of food helps them play their best, and that guides their choices at dinner and breakfast. Some like to play on an empty or nearly empty stomach, some don't. Some like to nibble energy bars or fruit during a round. Some like water and some like sports drinks. The important thing is to determine what works for you and stick to it.

Players generally try to get to the course a consistent time before they're scheduled to tee off. They need enough time to change, loosen up, and, if they're pros, take care of any press interviews or other matters. But they don't need a lot of time.

I believe that if you suddenly closed all the driving ranges and putting greens on PGA Tour golf courses from Thursday through Sunday, scores wouldn't change a whit. Players would stretch, take some practice swings, and hit the ball just as well as they do when they warm up for an hour. I recall that Billy Mayfair came to visit me in Virginia once when the weather was still cold and raw. Billy is from Arizona. He'd never played golf in temperatures below fifty degrees. It was too cold to warm up that day, with the temperature in the high thirties. We just stretched and played. Billy shot a 65. He was astounded, but I wasn't. Hitting balls before a round is overrated. You should do it just enough to warm yourself up and establish a good rhythm. Save serious practice for days when you're not competing.

## THOUGHTS TO PRACTICE BY

The only purpose of practice is to get you prepared for the most important shot of your life.

Make the practice experience as similar as possible to the competitive experience.

The week before a tournament is no time to make a swing change.

If a competition means a lot to you, you need a long-range plan to get ready for it.

Practice as you play. Play as you practice.

The warm-up before a competitive round is no time to panic over a bad shot and try to fix your mechanics.

# FOURTEEN

# PERFECTIONISM

O   O   O

*I stopped trying to do a great many difficult things
perfectly because it had become clear in my mind
that this ambitious over-thoroughness was neither
possible nor advisable, or even necessary.*
—Ben Hogan

It always gets my attention when I see perfectionist streaks in
the golfers I counsel. I am the first to acknowledge that many
great golfers have had perfectionist tendencies. I'll even con-
cede that the game probably demands a bit of perfectionism.
But perfectionism in a personality is like the seasoning in a
stew. A dash makes the stew rich and flavorful. More than that
can ruin it.

Perfectionist athletes tend to be highly motivated and dedicated. They refuse to accept limitations. They tend to set very
high goals and standards. What's wrong with that?

The problem is that their standards for the short term can be
too high. It's not a problem to have huge dreams. It's a prob-

lem when a player doesn't improve as quickly or as much as he thinks he ought to and refuses to accept imperfection. The perfectionist player gets angry and frustrated. Eventually, perfectionist goals and standards cause constant frustration and discouragement, which makes it hard to perform.

Perfectionists respond to this by putting more demands on themselves. They think the answer is to try harder and increase the quantity rather than quality of their effort. If that goes on long enough, their attitude deteriorates. They stop having fun at the game. They get lost in feeling sorry for themselves. At that point they'll start to question their commitment to golf. When they question their commitment, they usually feel guilty just for asking those questions. Soon they become overly critical of themselves. They're constantly berating themselves.

Perfectionists can become obsessed with their quest to eliminate error. Quite often this occurs with one of the critical clubs in the bag, the driver or the putter. I've seen players who can win hitting three-woods and long irons off the tee on tight holes instead take drivers. They hit the ball into trouble, and they ruin their chances to win. But they're obsessed with hitting perfect drives, and trying to do that becomes more important to them than winning.

The syndrome gets worse from there. The perfectionist can come to believe that the sports world is unfair. He can be filled with envy of players doing better than he is, particularly if he perceives that those successful players aren't working as hard as he is. He doesn't notice that the players he envies work smarter and more efficiently. The perfectionist increases the number of hours he spends practicing, but he's like Sisyphus struggling to roll a boulder up a hill. He keeps winding up where he started. His golf is consuming his life, and he measures his self-worth by the numbers on his scorecard. He has no hobbies. He sacrifices his relationships. He sacrifices everything for the game, and the game does not reward him. But he cannot imagine a better way to approach the problem. He is like a person stuck in a hole he's dug for himself, who thinks the solution must be to keep digging.

Understandably, the perfectionist finds himself feeling increasingly miserable. People don't want to be around him because he so often dominates conversation with complaints about how things aren't going his way. The perfectionist doesn't understand why people aren't patting him on the back and telling him how wonderful and different he is, praising him for his dedication. In competition he's paralyzed by anxiety and frustration. He can't learn from his experience. He pays no attention to its lessons. He rebuffs advice that backing off and accepting imperfections could lead to better results. He gets angry when someone suggests it.

Instead, the perfectionist thinks that the pain and the failure he's enduring are the price of success. It's understandable that he should think that way. As I said, golf demands a bit of perfectionism if you're going to be good at it. Golf lore is full of stories of players like Ben Hogan, who persevered through years of failure to develop a nearly perfect swing and dominate the game in the late 1940s and early 1950s. There's a very fine line between perseverance and constantly striving for improvement, and the debilitating form of perfectionism. It's when you go too far that you get into trouble.

If the perfectionism syndrome goes on unchecked, it can lead to mood swings, depression, increased anxiety, and reduced self-esteem. The perfectionist perceives all advice as critical. He gets defensive. That leads to more frustration and alienation from the people around him. Given that most perfectionists need the approval of others, they're really in trouble. They begin to believe, irrationally, that they must be more perfect to be accepted. They turn inward, they resist sharing their feelings, and they start to believe that human shortcomings won't be accepted. They can apply their own impossibly high standards to everyone else, becoming very judgmental of other people.

If you're concerned about your own tendency toward perfectionism, here's something you can monitor—your thinking. The thought pattern of the excessive perfectionist leans toward absolute, all-or-nothing judgments about himself and the way things are going. Either he's playing great, or he's playing awful. Either he's putting great, or he stinks at putting and he's always going to stink at putting. Either he's a great clutch player, or he has no guts. Many perfectionists are motivated by fear of failure, and this fear can overwhelm them. They begin to fear they'll never reach their goals. The perfectionist sees no grays. Anything less than perfect is a failure. He is tyrannized by the word "should." He should do better; he should work harder. He begins to think he's a bad person when he doesn't play well. He begins to feel he shouldn't be loved by those who love him.

If you're suffering from excessive perfectionism, your first task is to learn to like yourself. You need not accept limits on how good you can get, but you must accept the fact that you'll never be perfect and you may very well not be as good as you think you ought to be at any given moment. You have to learn to accept yourself and adjust to your imperfections. Where a perfectionist might tell himself, "I'm going to keep hitting this driver until I get it perfect," you might say to yourself, "I'll hit three-wood and get the ball in play."

You must separate your personal worth and feelings about yourself from how you perform on the golf course. You must be able to leave the course and enjoy yourself in the evening, regardless of how you played that day. Instead of driving yourself to master golf, drive yourself to master yourself, to be positive and encouraging of yourself all the time. Remember how lucky you are just to be playing golf, with an opportunity to practice, take lessons, and see how good you can get. Many people around the world don't have that opportunity.

You should banish the word "failure" from your vocabulary. There are setbacks in sports. They're part of the game. You'll have them. You've got to see your setbacks as an opportunity for growth and improvement. You may strive for perfection, but only with the understanding that humans can't be perfect and the game is really about seeing how close you can get. Learn how to do your best and feel no guilt when you fall short of perfection.

You must learn that one of the secrets to winning at golf is improving the quality of your misses. It's not eliminating misses, because no one does that.

You must learn that since no one is perfect, you need not be. I liked the way Hal Sutton pointed this out a few years ago when he won the Players Championship in a head-to-head battle with Tiger Woods at a time when Tiger seemed to be winning everything. "When I knelt down and said my prayers last night," Hal said, "I noticed I was praying to God and not to Tiger Woods. Therefore, Tiger must not be God."

Notice as you watch golf and other sports that athletes make mistakes. Watch how good athletes respond when they make them. Is there something they're doing that could help you?

Learn to dwell on your successes, however partial. Those thoughts will help breed more success. Dwelling on them is as important as practicing. Conversely, forget your mistakes. There's nothing productive about being ashamed or depressed. Take stock of your shortcomings and mistakes quickly, lay out a plan of improvement, then put them out of your mind.

Learn to take breaks. Perfectionists tend to think taking even a day off is a terrible sin. In their eyes, they're either dedicated, or they're lazy. Laziness is not a problem I find in perfectionists. Burnout is. Taking a break can refresh the well of desire, and enthusiasm rises.

Learn that your good friends are going to like you and value you for who you are, and not what you shoot. Don't spend your life expecting other people to understand or appreciate you when you're trying to be great and most of the world is trying to be average or fit in. They're not going to appreciate and understand you. Your good friends will if you give them a chance to see your desire as part of your personality, not an obsession.

Finally, don't worry too much if you've got a problem with perfectionism. It's fixable. In fact, it's a lot easier to fix than the opposite problem, which is the sort of personality that daydreams and talks about playing well, but is too lazy to do anything about it. That kind of person is very difficult to help.

## THOUGHTS TO PLAY BY

There is no such thing as perfect, so there are no limits. Because there are no limits, there is no such thing as perfect.

Perfectionism is like the spice in a stew. A dash is fine, but too much can ruin it.

Golf is by definition a game of mistakes, and if you think you must play perfectly, you either don't like golf or you think the other competitors are gods.

Improving the quality of your misses is important, but eliminating them is impossible.

Learn to take breaks and accept partial successes.

Banish the word "failure" from your vocabulary.

Rather than being a perfectionist on the course, you should play as if missing fairways and greens doesn't matter.

# FIFTEEN

# FEAR

O   O   O

*The only thing we have to fear is fear itself.*
—*Franklin D. Roosevelt*

There are two sorts of fear: the genuine kind, and the kind you may sometimes feel on the golf course.

Let's suppose that you were walking with your child at the zoo and a pride of lions somehow burst out of confinement and started running toward you and your child, looking hungry. You'd feel fear, the genuine kind, and you'd be right to do so. The fear reaction is one reason our distant ancestors on the African savannah managed to procreate before they became lion food. They passed this trait on to us.

Now let's suppose that you own the only golf course in the world and you're the only one who plays the game. No one watches what you do. Would you ever be fearful when you played?

You wouldn't of course. You'd have nothing to be frightened of. There are no hungry lions on a golf course.

So why, then, do some players feel fear when they play?

In golf, fear is usually rooted in worries about what other people will think of you if something untoward happens, be that a wild drive, a missed two-footer, or a shank. Fear can also be evoked if you know you will punish yourself for a mistake. If you are the sort to berate yourself all night for a missed two-foot putt, you have some reason to fear before you stroke it. But remember: Fear about golf is nothing more than a thought you have chosen to entertain.

Golf is a social game, and therefore it's inevitably associated with other people's opinions. Your play can evoke respect and admiration. It can persuade people that you have courage, that you're mentally tough, that you've got a good head. Unfortunately, it can also persuade them that you're clumsy and nervous.

But in the end, the absolute worst thing that can happen to you on a golf course is that you hit some bad shots, you don't win, and someone says something about you behind your back or to your face. It's a blow to your ego, nothing more.

Tom Kite once told me his daughter's gymnastics school amazed him. Every time those girls worked out or performed, they risked an injury that could paralyze them. They had reason to fear. But they didn't. The risk was so great that it forced them to put it out of their minds and perform coolly. Maybe if golf had that kind of risk, golfers would learn to be as clear-minded.

But there really is no danger in golf. In that sense it's like basketball, and something Michael Jordan once said is relevant. "Fear is like a mirage," Jordan said. "It's an idea you made up. It doesn't really exist."

If someone has a lot of fear on the golf course, it tells me he's spending a lot of time away from the golf course worrying about never being successful, worrying that he's working his tail off, putting in time and energy, and that he'll never be rewarded. He's fearful he wasn't destined to have great things happen to him.

I repeat the point that if you're going to think about golf, you've got to think about playing great. You've got to think about playing the way you want to play. It's okay to have occasional doubts, fears and worries. But you must not dwell on them. You want to recognize them for what they are and dismiss them. You've got to have the will and discipline not to allow yourself to brood about potential disaster, because the brain thinks that's what you want and that's what it's going to give to you on the golf course.

However, if you're ever on the golf course and a lion jumps out of the woods and starts running toward you, you have my permission to be afraid. Fear will help you run faster.

## THOUGHTS TO PLAY BY

You must realize that fear on the golf course is caused by an excessive concern about the opinions of others.

The worst thing that can happen to you on a golf course is a blow to your ego. That's nothing to be afraid of.

Throw away fear and play fearless golf, and your scores will drop.

# SIXTEEN

# COMMITMENT

O   O   O

*Golf is like life in many ways. For example, when*
*you make a decision, you should stick with it.*
—*Byron Nelson*

Here's a riddle I like to use with players (with apologies to vegetarians): "What's the difference between the pig's relationship to your bacon-and-egg breakfast and the chicken's relationship to it?"

The answer is that the chicken is involved in the breakfast. The pig is committed to it.

I use the riddle because commitment is an essential part of every great player's mindset. There are, in fact, two distinct types of commitment that every great golfer displays. The first is commitment to each shot. The second is commitment to a program of improvement.

On every shot, a golfer must have an image in his mind of how the ball will travel, and of the club and swing he'll use to get it there. Then he must commit to that image, decisively.

Otherwise, he can't hit the shot with a clear mind, and without a clear mind, the body is far less likely to produce a good swing.

Commitment means a narrow focus, a complete certainty about the shot, an unwavering mind, an absence of doubt, closure, and clarity.

Failure to commit can be just a bit of doubt or uncertainty. It could be that thought that wants to enter your mind as you address the ball: "Maybe I should cut a 6-iron instead," or "What if the putt runs six feet past the hole?"

If such thoughts plague you, it could be because you're not devoting enough time in your pre-shot routine to observing all the factors involved in a given shot. If you're addressing a putt and you suddenly notice the grain running away from you, and you didn't account for the grain when you were behind the ball, then your pre-shot routine was flawed. If you suddenly decide that your alignment is not good, that you're not aimed at the target, it could be that you're not being meticulous enough in your pre-shot setup. You need to address those issues in your pre-shot routine. You also need to back away from this particular shot until you can feel completely committed to what you're doing. Indecision will negate talent and skill.

Commitment is absolutely essential in difficult conditions like rain and wind. If you're not committed and decisive under those circumstances, you have no chance. The wind challenges your commitment. It gusts; it abates. It's easy to start changing your mind. In most cases, that's a mistake. You're better off following through with the shot you committed to, than you are trying to outguess the wind or wait for it to die down.

You've also got to be committed to the process of improvement. This can be different things for different players. If you're an amateur still struggling to break 90, it can mean following a schedule of lessons and practicing a few times between lessons. It can mean working every day on fitness. It can mean honestly evaluating the weaknesses in your game and turning your attention to them.

If you're a professional, your commitment may manifest itself in different ways. You already know the basic skills, though you may still have a commitment to honing your game and to attending regular sessions with a particular teacher. You also might have a fitness regimen that requires daily effort. If you have a teacher, you need to be committed to that teacher. You need to listen to him and only him for advice about your swing. You need to stick to the plan for improvement that you work out with your teacher.

You have more time than the amateur to practice, and you need a practice regimen. But at your level of development it's important to understand the distinction between being committed and trying to look committed. A player who is committed to the regimen that will make him his best understands that the quality of his practice may be more important than the quantity of his practice. He understands that working twelve hours a day, seven days a week, may not always be helpful to him. Indeed, that much time on the range can make a player stale and sloppy, especially just before a competition. For most players, it's ideal to taper off in practice before a competition, and to spend more practice time playing golf than hitting range balls. Players who understand the sort of commitment I'm talking about do everything that's necessary to prepare themselves. They do it efficiently. Then they do something else.

Some players are too concerned with demonstrating to others that they're committed. They are certain to be among the first on the range and the last to leave. They may spend a lot of that time schmoozing with other players. They may spend a lot of it mindlessly beating balls. But the media and the galleries think they're committed to improvement. They're not. They're committed to projecting an image.

A commitment is easy to make and hard to keep. If this were not so, more people would have scratch handicaps, taut waistlines and sufficient money in their 401(k) plans to retire at age 55. I find that people who keep their commitments tend to have an optimistic outlook. Their optimism buoys them when progress is slow or nonexistent. They're always thinking of reasons why they'll be successful in the long run. They believe that if they keep plugging away, something great will happen for them. People who are pessimistic tend to get discouraged in the face of adversity and give up.

Be an optimist!

# THOUGHTS TO PLAY BY

Commitment is an essential part of the
mindset of every player who strives to be great.

There are two types of commitment: commitment to a shot,
and commitment to a program of improvement.

Commitment to a shot means a narrow focus, a complete
certainty, an unwavering mind, an absence of doubt,
closure, and clarity.

Failure to commit before a shot can result from just a bit of
doubt or uncertainty.

It's more important to be decisive than it is to be correct.

Commit yourself completely to your plan for every
shot you hit.

Commit yourself to a program of improvement, and honor
your commitment.

# SEVENTEEN

# PATICE

O  O  O

*Maybe that is the answer—patience. Whatever I*
*may possess of it now must have been cultivated,*
*as I assuredly did not have it at first, and the*
*number of years required to hammer it into me*
*is a sorry commentary on my native intelligence.*
*—Bobby Jones*

Some players tell me they think they've got that patience thing
mastered because it's been a long time since they threw a club,
or cussed on television, or succumbed to the urge to find the
nearest tree and knock it over with their foreheads.

I'm sorry. That's not quite what we're talking about when it
comes to patience.

It is, perhaps, not coincidence that golf when it first came to
the United States was a sport of the moneyed classes. That's because golf is a game of leisure, a game of waiting, a game of patience. A hundred or more years ago, the rich were the only
ones in America who were skilled in leisure. They were the

only ones who could afford to be. The rest of the country worked six days a week and went to church on Sundays. That's obviously changed now. Golf is a sport for the millions, if not the masses. It's a sport played for money. But it is still a game of leisure, of waiting, of patience. It can't be forced.

The patience I'm talking about manifests itself in different ways at different levels of the game. During the final nine holes of the Masters, the patient player might be the one who can hear the roars from other parts of the course, see red numbers going up on the leader boards, and still not be tempted to go for the pin on No. 12. At your club on Saturday, it may be the guy who can be two down with four to play in a two-dollar Nassau, and still not try to hit a three-wood 210 yards over a pond to reach a par five in two strokes. Impatience may manifest itself in the guy who leaves a birdie putt inches short and can't wait any longer to see one go in. So he runs the ball nine feet by on his next birdie putt and winds up with a bogey.

At all levels of the game, patience means knowing that you can't dictate when success occurs. Great players like Jack Nicklaus, Nick Faldo, and Tiger Woods have tried to make their games peak for major championships, because they live to win those tournaments. Sometimes they can. Sometimes they miss the cut at the major; their game peaks two weeks afterwards, and they win the Buick Invitational instead of the U.S. Open. That's just how it goes.

At least Tiger, Nick, and Jack have lots of wins to think about when they need to be patient. It's tougher for golfers who have been working hard for a long time, trying to do all the right things, and still have not achieved their goals. Sometimes they ask me, "When is it going to happen?" I must answer that I don't know. I just know that if they're patient, and continue to do the right things, success will come. But golf cannot be forced.

All a golfer can do is his best. He can prepare himself and his game. When the time comes, he can play to play great. Beyond that, he has no control of the outcome. Someone may play better than he does. He may not be able to summon his best golf for a given tournament. In the face of this, he must be accepting.

To succeed, you must have an unshakeable belief that if you do the right things, wonderful stuff is going to happen to you. You can't control when.

A good golfer is prepared to take pride in the fact that he's got more patience than anyone else, that he can wait and wait for as long as it takes until the right opportunity presents itself to go for a flag or reach a par five in two. He knows that in golf, patience is rewarded.

## THOUGHTS TO PLAY BY

Golf is a game of leisure, a game of waiting, a game of patience. It can't be forced.

You can't dictate when success occurs.

A good golfer is prepared to take pride in his patience.

Expect good things to happen. Just don't expect them right now.

Success comes to the person who does the right things repeatedly and patiently.

# EIGHTEEN

# THE MYTH OF THE
# KILLER INSTINCT

O   O   O

*Most of the clubs we played against gave it their all
in the first half. When they found out they couldn't
dominate us, they lost their poise and character. It's
not that we play harder in the second half. We play
the same all the way through the game.*
*—Ray Nitschke, former middle linebacker,*
*Green Bay Packers*

Sportswriters, most of whom are not very good players, will
occasionally write that a winning golfer has the "killer instinct" or is a "great closer." As proof of that, they'll write
about how he can turn his intensity up a couple of notches during the last few holes of a tournament and secure the win.

Nothing could be more misleading.

The truth is that golfers win because they learn to attach the
same level of intensity and effort to every shot, whether it takes

place on Thursday morning or on the final hole on Sunday afternoon. They learn to downplay the importance of shots in critical moments. They learn to treat Sunday afternoon shots like practice round shots. It's the losers who try to ratchet their intensity up and play the closing holes as if they were the most important of their lives.

In my talks with different players, I've found that if you measured intensity of effort and desire on a scale of one to ten, most of them get their best results when their intensity is somewhere between three and six. If their effort drops too low, they tend to get sloppy. They might not focus on their target or set themselves up meticulously. But if their effort level gets too high, they get tight. They get mechanical. They might try to steer the ball instead of swinging freely. On top of that, when they're trying too hard, they get too analytical.

Brad Faxon has always told me that he putts his best when he doesn't care too much if he makes it. If he starts caring too much, he can't putt as well. That's another way of saying that when he just sees the ball going into the hole and hits it, when he's instinctive and intuitive, he's at his best. When he starts thinking and analyzing too much, his results suffer. Instead of trusting his first, instinctive read, he starts considering a second thought. The second thought is almost always the product of fear and nerves. It's rarely right.

Players tell me frequently how well they play when they're doing some kind of noncompetitive exhibition. They often play them on Mondays, generally with amateurs associated with one of their corporate sponsors. In this format, they play without worrying about their score. If they miss a shot or a putt, they shrug it off. Not surprisingly, they often shoot six or seven under par. Yet when they play in tournaments, they worry about their scores and how they're doing. They don't play as well. They'd be better off if they could bring the attitude they bring to client golf to tournament golf.

If you're a recreational player and you want an example of this, consider that staple of many an office outing, the scramble. A lot of people play their best golf in a scramble. Why? They're playing for a team, usually in front of friends, so they care enough. But they know that if they miss their shot, someone else on the team will likely hit a good one. So they don't care too much. They relax into that optimal level of intensity and they perform at their best.

This is an easy concept to enunciate, but not an easy one to practice. Davis Love III told me one of the things he noticed about himself during his highly successful 2003 season was that he felt he'd finally figured out his best level of intensity and learned to stick to it. For Davis, that level is about a four on the one-to-ten scale. Yours is probably somewhere close to that.

It's not always easy to get there because our culture trains people in some less-than-helpful concepts. One is that if you're not succeeding, you have to "try harder." This may be a useful idea in sports like cross-country running. It may be helpful to a student who needs to put more time into studying. But it leaves the impression that the right sort of effort is one that leaves you red-faced and panting, on the brink of collapse.

No one plays golf well if he's red-faced and panting. Golf is not a race. Nor is it war, or football. You can't get up a head of steam and hit someone. Golf is more like dancing. Look at Fred Astaire or Gene Kelly in an old movie sometime. The great dancers prepared meticulously and trained their bodies.

But when they performed, they simply listened to the music and responded to it. They didn't "dance their hardest." They danced their best.

Moe Norman, the Canadian golfer who has an intuitive and in many respects brilliant approach to the game, summed this up rather well. He said, "You have to play with detached indifference."

Baseball pitcher Mike Mussina gets it. A few years ago, he moved from the Baltimore Orioles to the New York Yankees. At his first spring training with the Yankees, reporters asked, "Mike, do you think you're ready to pitch for the Yankees?"

"Yeah. I've been pitching for years," he said.

"Mike, Yankee Stadium is going to be different. There'll be more pressure," the reporters persisted.

"It really doesn't matter what stadium I'm pitching in," Mussina replied. "I don't even notice what jersey I'm wearing when I'm pitching."

The writers couldn't accept this. (Among other things, reporters in New York take pride in the fact that *they* make it hard on athletes from the provinces.) "Mike, I tell you, you better get ready 'cause it's going to be different," one of them said.

"Let me explain," Mussina answered. "When I was a little kid and started pitching, my Dad painted a strike zone on the back of our barn in Montoursville, Pa. Every day as a little kid, I'd throw at that strike zone, pretending I was pitching in Little League, high school, college, or the pros. I was always imagining I was somewhere else when I was pitching to the barn. And when I pitched in big games, I pretended I was pitching to the strike zone on the barn. That's what I've always done, and that's what I'll continue to do. It won't matter who I'm pitching for."

I thought Mussina's answer was perfect. He refused to allow some outside agency—whether it be the New York press, the New York crowds, or George Steinbrenner—to affect the way he was going to pitch. He knew the level of intensity at which he pitched his best. He was going to pitch at that level, regardless of whether he was behind his Dad's barn or on the mound in Yankee Stadium.

Golfers have to be the same way. They have to find their most effective level of intensity and stay at it, whether they're chipping balls in their backyard or chipping to make birdie on the last hole of the U.S. Open.

## THOUGHTS TO PLAY BY

**Most golfers play best when their intensity level is mild to moderate.**

**Golf is more like dancing than it is war or football.**

**Don't try harder. Try your best.**

**Find your most effective level of intensity and stick to it on every shot.**

# NINETEEN

# THE RHYTHM OF THE GAME

O   O   O

*Playing golf you learn a form of meditation.*
*—Harvey Penick*

One of the great American amateurs of the last century, Bill Campbell, says he once learned a valuable golf lesson from Sam Snead. Campbell grew up in West Virginia, and when he was a teenager, he used to play pro-ams with Snead. One day he noticed that Snead whistled while he was walking the fairways. He asked Snead about it.

"Not only do I whistle when I'm playing golf," Snead said. "I always whistle a waltz."

Snead may have just liked waltzes. But there was something more to it. He recognized that the slow rhythm of a waltz would help his golf game. In those days, before videotapes and slow motion were widely available, golfers did not pay as much attention as they do today to the intricacies of swing mechanics. But they were keenly aware of rhythm and tempo.

I don't think it's a coincidence that a lot of the great players I've met from Snead's era had musical abilities. In those days, they'd often entertain themselves in the evening by gathering around a piano and singing. Most of them were great dancers. Rhythm and tempo were part of their lives.

Even today, when I talk to players privately, many of them will say that when a tournament is at stake and they don't want to mess themselves up by thinking of mechanics, they will think about rhythm and tempo. They're looking for a feeling of flow.

A good, gentle rhythm can be very helpful. A few years ago, when the U.S. Open was held at the Olympic Club in San Francisco, I took my dad out as my guest and arranged a round at the San Francisco Golf Club. My dad had never had a caddie, but for this round he had one. He was, naturally, nervous about it. In the middle of the round, I noticed he was chewing a big wad of gum.

"Dad, what are you doing with all the gum?" I asked. "My caddie gave it to me," Dad said. "He said chewing gum relaxes you."

A little while after that, I spoke with Riley Blanks, the daughter of an old Virginia basketball player, Lance Blanks, who is now the director of scouting and a color commentator for the San Antonio Spurs. Riley was a budding tennis star. Lance had once arranged for her to meet Michael Jordan. With a chance to ask Jordan anything, she asked him what he thought about during a time out. "What did he say?" I asked. "He said he just thinks about chewing his gum," the girl replied.

I'm not trying to endorse either the waltz or chewing gum.

But Jordan's answer brought to mind some meditation techniques that are designed to calm and clarify the mind. They have you focus on your heartbeat or your breathing. Chewing gum or whistling a waltz can serve the same function. If it establishes a good, languid rhythm, so much the better.

## THOUGHTS TO WHISTLE BY

**Feel free to use anything you find that can help you stay calm, languid, and rhythmic during a round of golf.**

# TWENTY

# ROUTINE

O   O   O

*Gee, when I'm concentrating and playing real*
*good, I can't think.*
—*Yogi Berra, answering a reporter who wanted*
*to know what he thought about when he was*
*playing well.*

The goal of a pre-shot routine is simple. It's designed to get you into the best possible physical position and mental state each time you swing at the golf ball.

People have different ideas of when their pre-shot routines actually start. Some players think their routine has begun as soon as they arrive at the ball and start gauging factors like the wind and the lie. Others think it begins after they've planned the shot and pulled a club, when they go behind the ball for a long look at the target. It's a matter of personal preference.

Whenever it begins, your routine has to accomplish the physical tasks of getting you into your stance and aligning your body toward the target. You can practice these movements in front of a mirror to make certain you're doing them consistently and properly. Nowadays, when golfers have been led to believe there is a perfect, scientific swing, they set great store in being aligned properly, on the theory that if the swing is perfect, the only thing that can cause a poor shot is poor alignment. Obviously, it's good to be meticulous about this, but it's not necessary to be obsessed with it. If you've practiced it sufficiently, you need to trust it. I see as many mental errors these days due to players worrying about their alignment as I see errors that stem from players worrying about their swings.

Some players have pre-shot routines that vary so little from shot to shot that you could use a stopwatch on them and the time they take would never vary. Other players have more flexible routines. They take more or fewer practice swings, depending on how long it takes for them to develop a clear mental picture of their shots. They are consistent only about the last phase of their routines, the time between that last look at the target and the initiation of the swing or stroke. Either way can work.

The most important part of your routine is the commitment it produces. By commitment I mean a complete absence of doubt about the shot you have planned and the club you're using. If you find yourself about to swing and wondering if you should hit a 5-iron or a 6-iron, you haven't properly executed your routine. If you find yourself about to swing and still unsure whether to hit your normal cut or a draw against a left-to-right breeze, you haven't properly executed your pre-shot routine. If you find yourself about to swing and uncertain exactly what your target is, or how the putt is going to break, you haven't properly executed your pre-shot routine. If you have properly executed your pre-shot routine, your mind is clear and decisive when you start your swing. You know exactly where you want the ball to go, how you want it to get there, and what club you want to use. If you don't know all of those things, you need to start your routine over.

You need to practice your routine just as much as you need to practice your golf swing. When you're on the range, imagine a fairway and go through your full routine, physically and mentally, just as if you were on the course. This will help greatly in taking your game from the range to the course.

Sometimes I see players who have great routines in practice and terrible routines in competition. Around the chipping green, for instance, they might have a very simple routine. They just look at the target, set themselves, and hit the shot. Not coincidentally, they chip very well in practice. When they get into competition, though, they think they need a very precise, sophisticated, and complex routine, as if they were checking off items for a space shuttle launch instead of a chip shot. It's not surprising that they get confused and tense when it counts.

When people tell me that they play better on the range than they do on the course, I want to know whether they employ the same routine on the course as they use on the range. Almost always, the answer is that they don't. On the course, they think more, they take more time, they're more careful. They get tighter. That's why they play worse. One of the first things I learned from my high school football and basketball coaches was that you practice the way you play, and you play the way you practice.

That applies to golf, too.

One obvious difference between practice and competition is that in competition you often must wait while other players play their shots. This complicates the task of emulating your practice routine, when you can rake a ball into place and start your routine whenever you're ready. The solution is to not think. You go brain-dead. You can learn to think about nothing until it's your turn to play. Or you can think about something unrelated to golf. It's not unlike what happened when I coached basketball and the opposing coach called a time out before one of my players shot a clutch free throw. In the huddle, I'd say something like, "Okay, after Jimmy makes his free throw, we're going to a full-court press" or whatever defense we were going to use. I'd spend the rest of the time out talking about defense.

You can keep a blank mind or think about whatever you want to think about until it's your turn. Then you go into your routine. And you play like you practice.

## THOUGHTS TO PLAY BY

A good pre-shot routine gets you into the best possible physical and mental state each time you swing.

Your physical routine must accomplish the task of getting you properly aligned and in the correct posture.

Your mental routine includes visualizing the shot and committing yourself to your plan.

Practice the physical elements of your routine until you can trust them in competition.

Use the same routine in practice that you use in competition.

Never hit a shot until your routine has produced an absolute commitment to that shot.

# TWENTY-ONE.

# YOUR BEST FRIEND
# ON THE GOLF COURSE

O  O  O

*You must not approach golf with a*
*single negative thought.*
*—Tommy Bolt*

Suppose, for a moment, that I was applying to work as your caddie. "What would you do for me besides carry the bag?" you might ask.

Suppose I answered: "First of all, whenever you hit a bad shot, I'm going to say, 'Terrible! That was terrible! How could you hit such a pathetic shot? You choking dog!' If you hit another bad shot, I'm going to get on you worse. 'You can't even play this game!' I'll yell. 'Why don't you give up?' Then, at night, I'll come to your room and remind you of all the mistakes you made that day. And the last voice you hear before falling asleep will be mine, saying, 'You stink!'"

You would, of course, tell me to go away and never come near you again.

I've noticed, in fact, that the most successful caddies on the pro tours, the ones with the longest tenure, are the ones who know how to do exactly the opposite of what I've described. They have a knack for giving their player words of encouragement, words that are framed in such a way that the player finds them credible. They don't sound like Pollyanna. But when the player needs to hear something positive, the good caddie gives him what he needs.

The first and last voice you hear on a golf course is not your caddie's, assuming you happen to employ one. It's the voice inside your head, the voice with which you talk to yourself. Are you giving yourself what you need?

Remember that your subconscious does not discriminate when it gets input from your conscious brain. If you're telling yourself that you're a lousy excuse for a golfer, the subconscious is going to accept that as true. If you keep telling yourself that you're a lousy golfer, the subconscious will start to believe that very firmly. Talking to yourself that way is like filling a trash bag full of garbage and carrying it over your shoulder while you play. No one would handicap himself that way.

Players tend to understand this when it comes to their own children. I know players who get tears in their eyes if you ask whether they'd ever berate or belittle their kids for hitting a bad golf shot. They're hurt by the very suggestion. If they walk with their children during a round of golf, they're constantly saying things like, "You can hit this shot, sweetheart. You're a good player."

Most people realize that they ought to tell a child what the child needs to hear, that they should calm down and speak patiently and kindly to their children if the child has misbehaved. Yet with themselves, they unload all their anger and frustration, telling themselves all the time how terrible they are. They think it's all right, even manly, to be tough on themselves. It's not all right. It's counterproductive.

You need to talk to yourself the way you'd talk to your own child. It's fine, after a round, to go over your scorecard briefly and decide that you need to work on a couple of aspects of your game that were less than you thought they should be. But while you're on the course, the inner voice you hear should be the one saying, "You can hit this shot, sweetheart. You're a good player."

## THOUGHTS TO PLAY BY

The last voice you hear on the golf course is your own.

It harms your performance if that voice is berating and belittling you.

On the golf course, your inner voice must talk to you the way you would talk to your child.

# TWENTY-TWO

# THE TEE

O   O   O

*There is no stroke in golf that gives the same*
*amount of pleasure as the perfect driving of the*
*ball from the tee.*
*—Harry Vardon*

Your mainstay tee club is a club that sets you up on any given hole to have a chance to score well. It's one of the clubs you have to love.

You have a choice. Maybe your mainstay club is your driver, or maybe it's a three-wood, a 1-iron, or a 2-iron. The important thing is not which club. It is the confidence that you can stand on the tee of the toughest driving hole of your life and know you can succeed. To succeed in competition, you must also be able to hit the ball far enough to be competitive at whatever level you play. If you can be that long with a 2-iron, that's fine. For most players, it's going to be either a driver or a three-wood.

The mainstay tee club is so important that a lot of golfers develop trouble with it. They understand its importance so well that they may develop fear about the consequences of mis-hitting with it. To overcome this you must, obviously, develop your skills. But there are plenty of players with the requisite skills who are nevertheless plagued by doubt on the tee. To overcome that you must develop a routine that emphasizes target orientation, that allows you to stay in love with your mainstay club and to trust it.

One big advantage in the psychology of the tee shot as opposed to, say, the psychology of the short game, is that off the tee there are always strategic options. With a wedge, you may not have options. There are times when you've got to pitch it over a bunker and stop it fast. You can't putt it or bump it. But off the tee, you can hit a three-wood or a long iron if that club makes you feel confident and will get the job done. There's no shame in doing this. It doesn't matter what anyone else thinks. It's smart golf.

I advise clients to stop looking at holes as draw holes, fade holes or straight ball holes. Your job, instead, is to see a way you can fit your ball flight into that hole's fairway. With very few exceptions, I think it's a mistake for golfers to think they should be able to hit a draw or a fade or a straight shot on demand in tense situations. They may be able to do this on the practice range. But in competition, it's almost invariably wiser to have a shot shape, be it draw or fade, that you use nearly all the time. I tell players that until they can step up on every hole, and absolutely trust their ability to hit a bread-and-butter shot, be it a draw, fade or straight ball, they shouldn't even think about curving it in different directions on different holes. If you can't do your favorite shot consistently, what makes you think you can do two or three? Find one shot shape and stick with it. If you get to the point where you're world class with it, my guess is you're not going to want to change it. In the tightest situations, you'll be glad you have a tee shot that's dependable, and you'll figure out a way to use it.

I want you to be in control of the golf ball. You have your favorite shot, and you own the golf hole. The course architect doesn't own you or your mind, and he doesn't dictate the shape of your shot. Neither does the wind. That's the right frame of mind on the tee.

Sometimes a player will object, "But, Doc, if the hole is a dogleg right and my bread-and-butter shot is a draw, I'll drive it too long and it will go through the fairway."

If that's the case, take another club. Don't let anything but your own game dictate the shape of your shot. I don't see any evidence that great players necessarily maneuver it both ways. I want you to go with the shot you know you can hit, your bread-and-butter shot.

On the tee, you must swing freely and confidently, but that doesn't mean swinging as hard as you can. Most players will be a lot better off if they stay within themselves. That means swinging at about 80 percent of your maximum force with the driver. That usually optimizes the chances of hitting the ball on the sweet spot of the clubface, which is the best way to get distance and accuracy. There's no percentage in swinging so hard that you lose your balance and rhythm.

Your commitment to advance planning for every important round will help you off the tee. You can never be certain what club you'll be using when you approach a green. But you can plan your tee shots in detail. I like players to come up to each hole having picked the target, the club, and the ball flight the night before. If they're playing a windy venue, they might have a couple of options in reserve, depending on what the wind is doing. This doesn't mean that the wind will dictate the curve of your shot; as we've discussed, it shouldn't. But if you come up to a dogleg and find a tailwind, you may want to play less club off the tee to fit your shot to the fairway. Vice versa if the wind is in your face. If the wind is quartering, it might affect the target line you select. What's essential here is that when you're walking to the tee, your thought process is simple. You see your shot, go through your routine, and hit the shot.

If there's any indecision once you've started your routine, walk away and start over. But there should not be if you've done the right mental rehearsal the night before, planning your shots and visualizing yourself executing them.

You want to have fun driving the ball, to love the first shot on every hole, to look at the tee box as a place you can get a huge edge on the field. But every good golf course has three to five tee shots designed to be very difficult. They will challenge you mentally, physically, or both. You must love knowing that you'll have your mind in the right place, trust your swing, and execute your routine on these holes. These holes are where you separate yourself from the competition. You don't beat people on the easy holes. You beat them on the tough driving holes.

While you understand the importance of hitting your tee shot accurately, you can't allow it to override your knowledge that the goal of the game is not hitting fairways. It's putting the ball in the hole. You must understand that it doesn't mean anything if you don't hit the fairway. You can score regardless of where you hit the tee shot. You must have just as much, or more, fun making birdies from the woods as you do from the fairway.

Golfers get into trouble, mentally, when they start becoming too concerned with the outcome of their tee shots—whether it's long or whether it lands in the fairway. Remember that you can only control how well you go through your routine. You can commit to having fun hitting tee shots.

And if you miss a drive, it's very important not to carry the memory to the next shot, or the next tee shot. Assume that the shot you missed was a fluke that won't repeat itself. Step onto the next tee as if it were the first tee and you've just come from hitting a bucket of perfect drives on the range.

## THOUGHTS TO TEE OFF BY

**Your mainstay tee club sets you up to score well on any given hole.**

**Off the tee, there are always options.**

**You must have at least one club in your bag that you can hit confidently on the toughest driving holes.**

**Don't let the hole dictate the shape of your shot. Stick with your own preference.**

**Swing freely, but don't swing as hard as you can.**

# TWENTY-THREE

# SCORING CLUBS

O    O    O

*If you're capable of hitting the ball close to the
hole, you're capable of shooting low scores.*
—*Tiger Woods*

The more I watch the best golfers in the world, the more convinced I become that what separates the great from the merely excellent is not the length of their tee shots. It's their proficiency with the scoring clubs. This is true at almost every level of golf beyond the beginner stage. Skill with the scoring clubs is the biggest difference between players who shoot in the 80s and players who shoot in the 70s. It's the biggest difference between pros and amateurs.

What are the scoring clubs? They're the ones you use to attack holes, to try to sink the ball. That means, for most players, the clubs from the 8-iron through the wedges, as well as the putter. Of course, anyone who plays a lot of golf understands the relationship between putting and scoring. Virtually anyone who's trying to improve knows he has to fall in love with putting. The importance of the other scoring clubs is not as widely known.

If you go, for instance, to one of the senior mini-tour events in Florida, you'll see a mix of players in their late 40s and early 50s trying to polish their games for the Champions Tour Qualifying School. Some of them are established professionals with a record of success on the PGA Tour. Some of them are players who turned pro in mid-life, chasing the dream of playing professional golf. Off the tee, you'll see surprisingly little difference between the pros and the erstwhile amateurs. But one place you will see a difference is in shots struck with short irons and wedges. The veteran pros almost always stick them close—within ten feet if it's a wedge shot. The erstwhile amateurs are just a little less sharp. They may put their wedges an average of 15 or 20 feet from the hole.

Every foot farther from the hole reduces a player's chances of sinking a putt. So the established pro, the one likely to go on to success on the Champions Tour, will make one or two more birdie or par putts per round than the guy who's likely to go back home and seek to regain his amateur status. That's a crucial differential in a professional tournament. The irony is that the erstwhile amateur will probably go home thinking that he lost to the veteran pro because his putter was cold while the veteran pro's was hot. He won't understand that the difference wasn't how well he putted. It was how close he hit his short irons to the hole.

Particularly for the shorter hitter, skill with these clubs is crucial. The shorter hitter can't start a round expecting birdies on the par-five holes because he can reach them in two shots.

But he can expect nine to twelve chances per round to knock a ball close to the hole with a short iron. He must capitalize on them. (Of course, so should the long hitter. As Tiger Woods has shown, the most devastating combination is a long hitter who's also deadly with his short irons and putter.)

There's no substitute for falling in love with these clubs and practicing with them until they become precision instruments for you. It may be sufficient, with a long iron, to be able to hit the ball long and straight. Skill with a scoring club must be more finely calibrated. A player has to know how to control the distance, trajectory, and spin of every shot he hits with them. If, for instance, he's going to shoot at a pin cut seven yards beyond a deep bunker and ninety-six yards from where he's standing, he's got to be able to hit the ball somewhere between ninety and ninety-three yards, have it skip once and stop. Eighty-eight yards won't do. Neither will a hundred yards. If the pin is on a shelf at the back of the green and it's one hundred and ten yards to the edge of the shelf and one hundred and twenty to the back edge, you have to be able to hit the ball one hundred and twelve yards, putting enough spin on it to stop it but not so much spin that it bites and rolls back to the lower tier.

As I've observed great players over the years, I've become convinced that skill with the long clubs determines how low your highest score will be, while skill with the scoring clubs determines how low your lowest scores will be. That's because if you can't put the ball in play off the tee, you're going to waste a lot of strokes. Hitting fairways regularly eliminates the really high score. But only if you are skilled with the scoring clubs will you make a lot of birdies and go low. With these clubs in your hands, your control must be such that you can take dead aim at almost any pin. You're trying to hole almost every shot you play with them, regardless of where the hole is cut.

This is a high standard of excellence. But I tell players that it's not unlike the challenge that faces a student who wants to go to medical school. C's and B's aren't good enough for him. If he wants to be a physician, he's got to make A's. If you want to be a scratch player or a successful pro, you can't settle for being merely good with the scoring clubs. You have to be better than good. You have to be dangerous with them.

# THOUGHTS TO SCORE BY

**You must fall in love with the scoring clubs and practice with them until they become precision instruments.**

**You must be able to fire at any flag with a scoring club in your hands.**

# TWENTY-FOUR

# SHORT GAME

O  O  O

*There's no need to tell anyone who has played a
great deal of championship golf that it's the short
game that decides the contests.*
—Tommy Armour

Quite soon after a player decides to improve, he or she inevitably confronts the short game. It doesn't take brilliance to
realize its importance. Even the best players miss one green out
of three, and for amateurs it's two out of three, or more. The
player who can get up and down consistently and chip in for
birdie occasionally is going to have a lower handicap and win
more often than the player who makes bogey or worse every
time a green is missed. I'm not the first person to notice this.
Anyone who studies golf can see that the big majority of
strokes are made within a hundred yards of the green.

Sometimes, when we discuss the importance of the short
game, a player will try to convince me that he doesn't have natural touch. In response, I hand him a ball. I step ten feet away

and ask him to toss me the ball. Invariably, he tosses it so that I can catch it easily, just in front of my body. I change the distance, stepping back another ten feet or moving close, to five feet. The player instantly adapts to the new distance, and the tosses remain soft and easy to catch.

"You have natural touch," I tell the player. "You're just not bringing it to your short game for some reason."

Sometimes the problem is that the player is too worried about making crisp contact to pay attention to his target. Maybe he's skulled a chip under pressure, or chili-dipped it. If you're worried about doing those things, you won't have touch. Your brain will be trying desperately to force your body to make clean contact with the ball. Of course, thinking consciously and desperately about making clean contact is a good way to rob your body of its natural rhythm, grace, and skill. It will promote, rather than diminish, the chances of another skull or another fat shot. And if you do hit it crisply, you'll have little better than random chance that the ball will get to the target, because in executing the shot you won't have the target in mind.

If a player has a mechanical flaw that affects his chips and pitches, I'm the first one to tell him to see a good swing teacher to correct the flaw. If he has no time for that before his next competitive round, I generally offer a few ideas that any good swing teacher would suggest: Keep most of your weight on your left foot (for right-handers); position the ball toward the back of your stance at address; get the hands in front of the ball at address so the handle of the club is closer to the target than the clubhead is; and maintain that shaft angle through impact. I know players who have struggled successfully with short-game nerves by remembering these four principles. Under pressure, they respond by exaggerating them—keeping more weight on the left side, getting the hands farther ahead of the ball, playing it farther back in their stances and tilting the handle more toward the target. This assures crisp contact and allows their natural touch to emerge. I see accomplished players on the professional tours resort to this all the time when they're feeling shaky about their short shots. They get through the round with it. They work to correct their form after the round.

I also tell players facing competition and worried about their short games not to be concerned about the club they use. There are situations where putting the ball from the fringe or bumping it with a three-wood are perfectly efficient ways to get the golf ball to the hole. Players are afraid to do this because they think a good player is "supposed" to hit a wedge from around the green and they're worried that people will think less of them if they don't use a wedge.

I don't understand this. When Tiger Woods bumps a three-wood around the green, people think it's cool. When Phil Mickelson putted several times from off the green and won the Masters, they didn't deny him the green jacket because he was "supposed" to hit wedges. When I watch Brad Faxon play a practice round before a tournament, he frequently drops a few balls off a green and takes his wedge, his putter, and his four-wood with him. He experiments to find out which club works best on that course, as the grass is cut that week, and what might work best when it's wet and soft or when it's dry and firm. Brad has one of the best short games in golf, and he'll use whatever club will get the job done for him. But, still, some players feel compelled to play the "classic" shot, even if it means using a club they're not confident with.

That violates a cardinal rule. If you're not confident that you can hit the shot you want with the club in your hands, get another club or plan another shot. Never hit a shot in doubt.

These, however, are short-term, stop-gap responses to get around a problem that has to be resolved. To resolve the problem, there are four things you must do:

First, fall in love with the short game, and with your short game. Recognize that short shots are an integral part of the game you love, and that you love them just like you love your spouse's crooked little smile. (I realize that the list of golf elements I advocate falling in love with is growing. If you feel your supply of love getting stretched thin, you have my permission to remain lukewarm about your long irons.)

Second, reconstruct your short-game self-image. You begin by thinking about hitting great chips and pitches. Then you start taking great pleasure and pride in successful short shots. And why shouldn't you? There's something terrific about clipping a ball just right from off the green, watching it hit the putting surface, skip and check as the backspin takes hold, then roll slowly to the hole, stopping next to it like an obedient dog—or plopping in. Celebrate such shots. The pleasure you feel will help cement the memory of them in your subconscious.

You can accelerate the reconstruction by keeping a record of your best short shots. Tour pros get videotape of their best moments. The rest of us can write them down in a notebook or computer file dedicated to that purpose. Consult the tape or the book frequently to help reinforce your good memories. Remember that your short-game self-image is composed of all the thoughts and memories you have of yourself chipping and pitching. The more recent and intense memories are the stronger ones. With patience, persistence, and the right approach you can build an image of yourself as a deft, confident player around the greens.

Work on this in your interactions with other players. When people ask how your game is, tell them your short game is doing fine. Don't hang around with people who moan about their own short games. Bad chippers are going to complain about how tight the turf is cut or how hard the ground is. You don't want to be drawn into their self-pity. This is a corollary of Harvey Penick's old admonition about not going to dinner with bad putters.

When you hit a bad short shot—and everyone does—forget it. You need amnesia for such moments.

Third, you must practice, especially with shots that bother you. If you have trouble with tight lies or bare lies, then you need to find something like a dirt cart path or an expanse of hard pan and practice off it. Hit from old ball marks or the sand in old divots. Lob over mounds from tight lies. You can be certain that if there's a shot you particularly dislike and you don't practice it, you'll face that shot at a critical moment in competition. Golf has a way of doing that.

Fourth, you have to stop caring and berating yourself when you miss a green. Missing a green only means that you've got a chance to make birdie or par the adventurous way. Too many players invest enormous emotions in hitting the green. When they don't, they get upset. Players with good attitudes about their short games don't get upset. They figure that everyone's going to miss some greens, and skill at recovering from those misses is one way in which they can separate themselves from the competition. Instead of worrying about a bogey, think of how much fun it will be to chip in, or save par, and how devastating it will be for your opponent if it's match play. Nothing deflates an opponent more than losing a hole he'd mentally put in his pocket.

Finally, from around the green, you must always chip or pitch to make it. You're not trying to get it close. You're trying to hole it.

Nothing will give you more pleasure than mastering your own insecurities about the short game and turning it into a facet of golf that helps you score and win.

## THOUGHTS TO CHIP IN BY

The player who can get up and down consistently is going to have a lower handicap and win more often.

Everyone has adequate natural touch.

Your touch can't help you if you're worried about making crisp contact.

Fall in love with your short game and, if necessary, reconstruct your short-game self-image.

Use whatever club works to get the ball in the hole.

Practice the short shots till you're absolutely confident with them.

Stop caring and berating yourself when you miss a green.

Chip or pitch to make it.

# TWENTY-FIVE

# PUTTING

O  O  O

*Kids have no fear when they putt. They miss it and*
*it doesn't affect them. You've got to keep that atti-*
*tude your whole life. That's my whole premise*
*toward putting. If you care whether you miss,*
*you're in trouble.*
—Brad Faxon

I have a friend, Bill Heron, who is the head professional at
Meadowcreek Golf Club, near my home. Bill has a great attitude about putting. He tells me that when he walks onto a
green, he feels like he's arrived at an oasis after a long trek
through the desert. On the green, he's safe and secure.

Bill has discovered a way of doing what any golfer who
wants to be good must do. He's found a way to fall in love with
putting. If you want to be a great golfer, you've got to feel that
putting is where the fun begins. You've got to feel that it's party
time when you step onto a green. You've got to walk onto a

green feeling, "Ah, finally we get to putt! This is where I show off!"

If you can feel this way, you'll have a big edge on misguided competitors who think that putting is somehow a lesser skill than driving the ball or hitting irons. There have always been players who thought this way, who wanted putts to count half a stroke or who wanted to enlarge the size of the cup to make putting skill less critical. They've always been wrong. The objective in golf is to put the ball in the hole. That's something golfers accomplish, 90 percent of the time or more, with their putters. Putting is the heart of golf. The shots we make with the long clubs are essentially just an overture to the act of putting.

But there's a paradoxical quality to putting. At the same time as good putters recognize the centrality of putting, they refuse to get too concerned over the fate of any single putt. The good putters have gotten rid of thoughts like, "You have to make this one," or "You ought to make this one." They treat every putt the same, whether it's a ten-footer for a birdie to win a tournament or a four-footer to save bogey on Thursday morning. It's still, to them, just a putt. Only two things can happen to it. They can make it or they can miss it. They know that in either case, the sky will not fall around them and the earth will not open and swallow them up.

Consequently, good putters never putt out of fear. Whatever length their first putt is, they aren't worried about how long their second putt is going to be. They're going to try to make the first one. They may want the first putt to plop into the hole on its last revolution, if it's a long, slippery, downhill putt.

They may want the ball to bang against the back of the cup if it's a straight, uphill putt. But whenever they putt, they have only one objective, to put the ball in the hole. If you find yourself worrying about three-putting, your mindset needs an adjustment. If you find yourself thinking, "Unless I make this birdie putt, I'll have wasted two good shots," your mindset needs an adjustment.

Good putters realize that they can't control whether the ball goes in the hole. They can only control their own thoughts and actions. Dana Quigley once told me a story about himself and Brad Faxon. Dana watched Brad play a round in Florida and to Dana it seemed that Brad was hitting his long shots well but missing a lot of putts. After the round, he saw Brad and said, "Nice round. If you'd just putted decently, you'd have had a great day."

"What are you talking about? I putted great out there," Brad replied. "You've got to be kidding," Dana said. "Well, I'm sorry, but I loved how I putted today," Brad insisted.

It was not until we discussed it that Dana understood what Brad meant. Brad is one of the world's best putters, and one of the reasons for that is he doesn't judge his putting by how often the ball goes in the hole.

A good putter has certain goals when he putts. He wants to trust his first instinct about how the ball will break. He wants to "see it and do it." By that I mean he sees the target and lets the stroke go without any intervening thought. He wants to trust that his stroke will roll the ball where he's aiming it. If he does all of those things on all of his putts, he figures he's had a good day. He's "made" all his putts, mentally. He knows that if he makes all his putts mentally, in the long run he's also going to make a lot of putts in actuality. And he does.

Let's review those objectives.

First, he wants to trust his first impression when he reads a green. I am often told by professional clients how well they read greens during pro-am rounds when their amateur partners ask for help. They take a quick look and say something like, "It'll break two cups to the left if you hit it medium speed." The amateurs quite often finish the round thinking that their professionals are geniuses at reading greens.

They are—when they trust their first impression. Unfortunately, in competition, too many players think they have to work harder at reading greens. They feel guilty if they don't ponder the problem for as long as the rules allow, and from as many angles as they can imagine. Two things tend to happen as a result. They overread the putts, seeing breaks that aren't there. In overreading and changing their minds, they undermine their trust in what they see. If it was wrong the first time, why can't it be wrong the second and third times?

It's always best to trust your first impression. You can take in all of the necessary information, about slope, grain, and speed in a short time. Once you've done that, stop reading the green.

Second, a good putter tries to "see it and do it." It's remarkable how different players can be when it comes to the first part of that formulation. Some players see, in their mind's eye, a line on the green that demarcates the path the ball will take. Some see a variation of that—railroad tracks, for instance. Some people see funnels, and some see laser devices. Some see a preview movie of a ball rolling into the hole. And some get no visual image. They have an abstract notion of how the ball will behave. But all good putters get a strong sense of how the ball will roll into the hole.

Third, the good putter always putts to make it. He doesn't try to get it close. He wants the ball to go in. Sometimes, if it's a slippery, downhill putt, he wants it to plop into the hole on its last revolution. Sometimes, as on a short, straight, uphill putt, he wants to bang it against the back of the cup. But he never lags the ball. He understands that if he's trying to make it, he'll get it closer than he would if he were trying to leave the ball within a three-foot circle.

But this doesn't mean the good putter tries to "force" it in or "will" it in. Nor does it mean he gives himself a seminar in positive thinking as he stands over the ball. It means he strokes the putt freely. He assumes it will go in, and he doesn't fear a miss.

Players differ in how long the image of the target and the path the ball will take to get there are retained in the mind's eye. Some players, like Nick Price, can "see" it for quite some time, almost as if his brain was a digital camera holding an image. Others, like Brad and Davis Love III, see it only fleetingly. This affects a critical stage of their putting routines. Nick can take more time between his last look at the target and the initiation of his stroke. Brad and Davis take less. Your routine should be determined by the same consideration. The critical factor is that you react to your target and the vision you have of how the ball will get there.

When Davis and I discussed this, he immediately saw a couple of parallels. He's taken trap shooting lessons. The teacher advised him to never let the gun be still. He didn't want Davis consciously to try to aim it. Instead, he wanted Davis to keep the barrel of the gun in motion, to look ahead of the target and react. He wanted a fluid, instinctive shot. The concept also reminded Davis of a little desk toy he'd seen in the airport in Atlanta, the one with five balls that stay in motion. As soon as one ball hits the row of balls, the one on the opposite end caroms off. That was the way Davis felt about his putting routine when he was at his best. He takes a look at the target and returns his eyes to the ball. His putter draws back as instantaneously as that silver ball caroming off the row of balls. It's a matter of seeing the target and reacting to the target, fluidly and instinctively.

When you simply "see it and do it," you don't worry about speed. You trust that your brain will adjust to the greens you're putting on. Fifteen minutes on the practice green should be all you need to adjust naturally. It's a mistake to go out on the golf course thinking, "These greens are slow; I have to putt harder," or vice versa. Just spend the time required on the practice green and let the speed happen. You might, if you find the greens are inordinately fast or slow, think about having the ball dribble over the edge of the cup or hit the back of the hole. But don't think about hitting your putts harder or softer. Think about putting the ball into the hole.

Fourth, a good putter knows better than to be influenced by how his first few putts go. There are many players who don't. If they don't make a putt on the first few greens, they start to fight themselves. They decide that it's not their day, or there's something wrong with their stroke. The good putter, on the other hand, understands that if he gets off to a good start, it means he has to keep doing what he's been doing if he wants to go low. If he gets off to a poor start, it means he has to keep do-ing what he's been doing and expect that the breaks will even out and he'll make some birdies.

Finally, the good putter strives to trust his stroke. He's worked hard on it over the years, though he knows better than to work at it on the golf course. He knows that it's not a very complicated movement. More important, he knows that if he starts thinking about the mechanics of his stroke, he's going to interfere with the connection between the picture in his mind and the stroke. The stroke is something that happens in re-sponse to the image you have in your mind. In competition, the best putting strokes are unconscious putting strokes. A key principle to understand is that you gain control by giving up control. When players understand that, they almost invariably start hitting the ball more solidly, in the middle of the putter face. That improves the consistency of their putting.

The good putter's overall putting routine need not be the same from one green to the next. That's because sometimes it takes him more or less time to come to the firm conviction that he understands the line and speed that will deliver the ball to the hole. The important thing is that he comes to a firm com-mitment about his putt before he addresses the ball. He doesn't stand over the putt exhorting himself. He knows that if he's doing that, he hasn't executed that part of his routine that oc-curs before he addresses the ball. Before address, he decides what he thinks the putt will do. He commits to that decision.

At the critical moment, though, the good putter's routine never varies. He looks at the target. He sees the ball going into the hole. He lets the stroke go. If he does all of those things properly, he considers the putt "made," regardless of what the ball actually does. That's why a good putter can feel he putted well on a day when not many long ones fell.

Of course, when you do all these things right in the long run, anyone watching is going to see a lot more putts disappear into the hole.

## THOUGHTS TO PUTT BY

**Putting is the heart of golf.**

**Great golfers feel that the putting green is where the fun begins.**

**Good putters never putt out of fear.**

**Instinctive impressions are better than second and third reads.**

**A good putting routine is one where you "see it and do it."**

**Speed happens.**

**You must trust your stroke.**

**Always putt to make it.**

**Putt as if it doesn't matter if the ball goes in.**

**Never address the ball until you've first seen it go in.**

**Never let missing the first few putts alter your mindset or routine.**

**Never care if you miss.**

**Love one-putting more than you fear and loathe three-putting.**

# TWENTY-SIX

# SETBACKS

O  O  O

*Any fellow who has a good shot has got to take it*
*and keep taking it. So he misses. So what?*
—Red Auerbach

Once in a very great while, I see someone enjoy a smooth ride to the top. In golf, Tiger Woods and Jack Nicklaus come to mind, although Jack "endured" six months of missed cuts and small checks before he won his first professional event, the 1962 U.S. Open.

The rest of us have to cope with setbacks and failures. Golf is a game in which many of the key factors are beyond the control of an individual player. He can't control how well his opponents play. He has only imperfect control of his golf ball. Even near perfection in shotmaking can be rewarded with an ugly bounce into trouble. Ask any U.S. Open competitor who's seen a great iron shot into a green hit a particularly dry, hard knob and bounce into jail. A golfer can influence, but not control, the state of his own game. If there were a sure way to tune a game through practice, then everyone would show up at the Masters or his club championship with his game at its best. In reality, few players do.

If golf had an inventor, you would have to say that he designed it to produce failures. If you ask a good veteran player at any club to list the best score he's ever made for each hole at his club, the total will probably be somewhere in the 50s. Most people who play a course regularly have birdied all the holes at least once and eagled a few. The same player with this "ringer" score of, say, 52, probably has a career best round in the 70s. So even on the best day of his life, a good golfer has probably been at least 20 strokes away from his proven potential.

The competitive structure of the game adds to the inevitability of failure. In golf, one player wins each tournament. In football, half the players win on any given weekend. In golf, half the players miss the cut and don't get paid. In baseball, even a player in an 0-for-20 slump gets a check.

The game will try to beat you up. You'd better not be beating yourself up as well. Any golfer must learn to bounce back from failure.

You don't bounce back by dwelling on your mistakes. American culture subscribes to the myth that improvement comes about through rehashing mistakes, dwelling on them, brooding over them. It's a destructive myth. It is useful to take a quick look back, identify what went wrong and, if possible, fix it. But it needs to be a quick look. Ten minutes should be enough. And it won't help to get obsessed with eliminating a weakness.

Suppose, for instance, a player looks back on failure and decides that it was due to the fact that he didn't drive the ball far enough to reach the par fives in two strokes. He throws himself into the quest for more length. He tries swing adjustments. He tries new equipment. He may get marginally longer, but it's not likely that he'll get better results, because he's been neglecting his scoring clubs. The truth of the matter is that it's very rare for a golfer to turn a weakness into a strength. A good player can work on a weakness and eliminate it, even become good in that aspect of the game. But you win by maximizing your strengths. Obsessive attention to what seems to be the cause of a setback won't help you do that.

When you fail, it's important to have some compassion for yourself. That doesn't mean you go into denial about the fact that a failure has occurred. It means that you accept the failure, learn what you can from it, and forgive yourself for it. That shouldn't be impossible to do. You're a human being, born flawed, and you're going to make mistakes. The best thing you can do is let your mistakes go and forget about them. If you can't do that, you'll fill your mind with thoughts of bad shots. You need to be filling your mind with thoughts about the best golf you can play in your next round.

Refusing to get upset about bad shots can help you. If you get enraged every time you mis-hit a ball, your mistakes will linger longer in your memory. They'll affect your self-image and confidence longer. It's best to discipline yourself to accept mistakes phlegmatically and move on.

There is one thing you can control in golf, and that's your attitude. There are going to be days when your attitude is all you can be proud of. I have a friend who plays in amateur tournaments in Virginia. Recently he hit his first tee shot in an event and thought he hit it well, down the right edge of the fairway. He figured he'd find it either in the fairway or barely in the rough. When he got out to the landing area, he couldn't see it, but he wasn't worried. There was a marshal there specifically to locate tee shots. He asked the marshal where his ball was. "I didn't see it," the marshal said.

My friend looked for his allotted five minutes and couldn't locate his ball. He had to walk back to the tee and hit another drive. In effect, he had spotted the field two strokes. There is no walk in sports more ignominious. As he walked, my friend thought about how he was going to react. He realized he couldn't be mad at the marshal. He was just a senior citizen volunteering for a job my friend wouldn't want to do. He couldn't get mad at himself—he'd hit a good drive.

He decided that the best thing he could do was try to make birdie with his second ball. And he determined that no matter what else might go wrong, all the people he contacted that day would have reason to talk over dinner about how good his attitude had been in the face of adversity. That attitude helped. He bounced back to shoot even par for the day.

When you maintain a good attitude, setbacks don't bother you much. They make an impression like a big truck passing on a two-lane road. It's soon dwindling in the rearview mirror. You're focused on the road ahead.

When your attitude is bad, you dwell on your setbacks. You're not good company for your friends and family in the evening. You wallow in self-pity. You lose yourself in the work of worry.

If you wonder how your attitude measures up, ask yourself this question: How would you respond to a setback if God had already told you that you were going to play the round of your life, or win the tournament, or win three tournaments this season? If you hit a drive out of bounds on the first hole, you'd think, "Well, that's interesting. I guess I'm going to make a lot of birdies the rest of the way in." If you played the first nine holes of the tournament four over par, or four over your handicap, you wouldn't get upset. You'd just assume that you were going to get very hot very soon. And if you missed a couple of cuts in a row, you'd think that the experience was going to make your three victories all the sweeter.

I don't know of anyone who's had a Divine Revelation about a round of golf, or a tournament, or a season. But I know many players whose attitudes would be much more helpful to them if they were convinced that they had.

## THOUGHTS TO BOUNCE BACK BY

The nature of golf is such that everyone must cope with setbacks and failures.

Dwelling on failures compounds the initial mistake.

When you maintain a good attitude, setbacks don't bother you too much.

Have compassion for yourself when you fail.

Refuse to get upset about bad shots or bad tournaments.

Take pride in the way you bounce back from setbacks.

Play as if God has told you that you were going to win this tournament, or win several tournaments this season.

# TWENTY-SEVEN

# VISUALIZATION

O   O   O

*I know that I have sometimes concentrated so hard on the shot I was going to hit that I honestly felt that the shot could not fail to come off exactly as I intended. On those occasions, I had the definite sensation that I had really hit the shot before I even started my club back.*
—*Ben Hogan*

One of the questions golfers most frequently ask me is "How am I supposed to be confident I can win if I haven't won yet?"

There are many answers. Some players manage to carry the confidence they gained at a lower level to a higher level of competition. Tiger Woods comes to mind in this regard. When he turned professional and began to play on the PGA Tour, did he retain the confidence he'd built from his success in junior golf, collegiate golf, and national amateur tournaments? I believe he did. Ben Curtis's first win at the big league level was the British Open. But he corrected reporters who said it was his first professional win. He'd won on the Hooters Tour. It was clear that he'd carried confidence from that tour to Royal St. George's.

There's another avenue to early confidence, one available to every golfer, regardless of past record. It's visualization. You can mentally rehearse performing well and winning. If you do it properly, you can give yourself a feeling of *déjà vu* when you're in a clutch situation. You can make yourself think and perform like the successful veteran who doesn't get distracted by competitive pressure because he knows he's been there before and he's handled it.

I'm speaking of visualization. You can write an imaginary script for the way you want to perform. You can perform that script in your mind. It can give you much the same state of calm assurance the successful veteran has.

That's because the human organism only dimly perceives a difference between a vividly imagined event and the real thing. For proof of this, consider nightmares. People who have nightmares may see themselves driving a car off a cliff, to take one possibility. They awaken terrified, with adrenalin flooding their bodies, just as they would be if they really were in a car flying off the road and over a cliff.

A nightmare is an involuntary expression of the subconscious mind. It's a little more difficult to make an image that you consciously create affect the body so powerfully. A simple daydream isn't going to have such an impact. But you can go well beyond daydreaming in your visualization.

To begin with, get yourself in a very relaxed state. Lie down if possible. The more relaxed you are, the clearer the pictures in your mind will be. Put yourself in a place with no distractions. A darkened bedroom is ideal. You can have some background music if that relaxes you.

Now begin to create your scenario. The images in your mind may take the form of pictures your eyes would deliver to your brain if you were living your imaginary scenario. Or they could be like television images of you from a slight distance. They might not even be particularly visual. Some people have less graphic images than other people. Their imaginary story can unfold like a novel rather than a movie. Reading a book can be just as vivid an emotional experience as watching a movie.

What's important is that your imaginary experience feels real. It should be happening in the present moment, rather than some time in the future. Involve all your senses. Smell the grass and the flowers. Feel the breeze on your face and the club in your hands, the ground under your feet. Listen to the birds. Experience the sounds of the crowd—their hush before a shot, their polite applause, their birdie roars. Take in the entire visual panorama of the setting. If you're imagining a major championship, see the flags flapping in the wind. See the photographers crouched inside the ropes. See the hospitality tents on a hillside and the grandstands and television towers around the greens. If you're thinking about a club championship, see that setting: the clubhouse, the pro shop, the golf course. Regardless of the level of competition, envision the golf course in great detail. See the fairways and the bunkers, the greens and the pins.

Most of all, see yourself hitting great shots. Some people tell me that when they attempt this exercise, they envision themselves hitting bad shots. If that happens a lot, it's testimony to the high concentration of fear and doubt in your mind. It means you need visualization exercise all the more.

That's not to say that the ideal visualization session will have you shooting 54 in every round and winning the tournament by dozens of strokes. On the contrary, you should envision difficult scenarios. Imagine yourself two strokes back with two holes to play. Imagine yourself caught and passed midway through the final round by another player, then fighting back. Imagine yourself tied and going into a playoff, where the opening hole requires a long drive fitted between water and deep rough.

Do all of this in great detail. The more vividly you can see yourself passing such tests—hitting the crucial drive, making the slippery five-footer, chipping in for an unlikely birdie when it's most needed—the more likely you are to experience the real thing. It's not just the sense of *déjà vu* that will bolster your confidence when you actually find yourself in a clutch situation. Visualization exercises will improve your ability to focus, to shut out distraction, and to concentrate on what you want to achieve.

You can use this sort of visualization exercise to help you with a range of issues that arise in golf. It can help you overcome a "barrier" like breaking 90 or 80 or 70. If you're a professional, it can help you cope with a tendency to hit the brakes when you make a few early birdies. It can help you go low.

You can think of this as "mental practice" if that terminology makes you more likely to consider it an essential part of your preparation for competition. Obviously, you can't prepare solely with mental practice. You need to work on your physical skills. But mental preparation is at least as important as physical preparation. Everything science has learned about sports performance suggests that a combination of physical and mental preparation works best.

I learned about the power of this technique before I started working primarily with golfers. As director of sports psychology at the University of Virginia, I helped the football and basketball programs break barriers and achieve goals that had eluded their predecessors. The 1983–84 basketball team remains a proud example.

There were no budding NBA all-stars on that team. It was a group of future attorneys and financial analysts that tried to slow down the pace and play smart basketball. We were seeded seventh in the Eastern Region, considered a team that might get through one round but would certainly not make it past that. The powerhouses in the bracket were North Carolina, Arkansas, and Indiana.

That Virginia team, though, relished the role of underdog. It played with poise in tight games. We squeaked by Iona in the first round, 58–57. In the next round, we upset Arkansas, 53–51. We dispatched Syracuse in the regional semis, 63–55, and then faced Indiana for the right to go to the Final Four.

Before each game, we used visualization exercises. I would gather with the coaches and players in a hotel suite. We'd unplug the phones. The players would stretch out on the floor. I'm going to reproduce here the script I used the night before the Indiana game because it gives a good sense of how a visualization exercise is structured. Remember as you read it that it was designed to help the players *see* themselves performing. My words were a stimulus for their imaginations.

*Get in a relaxed position, on your stomach or back. As
I turn the lights low, slowly and softly close your eyes.
Imagine it's a warm summer day and feel the sun shine*

*down on your body. Your body feels warm and heavy as the heat of the sun soaks in. It feels good to be warm and relaxed. You're in a favorite place where you feel comfortable, warm, and at ease. Enjoy the feeling. Breathe very deeply and slowly. Inhale. Count to four. Exhale, and count to four. Repeat that a few times. Be relaxed enough to have control of imagery, but not so relaxed you go to sleep.*

*Let's focus our minds on playing Indiana. Tomorrow's game at the Omni is for a trip to the Final Four. They're the favorite. This is to our advantage. All the pressure is on them. We have everything to gain, nothing to lose. Let's utilize the opportunity. We can get the crowd behind us as underdogs. If Indiana gets in trouble they might get frustrated. We are composed.*

*The first step is to remember to get to bed early tonight and get a good night's sleep. You've worked for years to be ready for this day, so let's be prepared to play hard for forty minutes, or more if the game goes into overtime. We play early tomorrow, at 1:30 p.m. A key will be our readiness for the opening tap. Let's wake up early at 7:30, feeling rested, ready, wide awake, knowing we're ready to play a great game. Be on time for the pre-game breakfast and be ready to listen to the scouting report one last time.*

*Now let's totally concentrate on the game. Make it as if we were playing it right now. Feel yourself in the locker room. Smell it. Put your uniform on and carefully put your shoes on and lace them up. Take a ball and go out to the court on your own. See the first spectators coming in. Feel the excitement. Your dreams are coming true. Get a feel for the court. Find the soft spots. Get used to looking at the basket and the crowd in the background. Feel the tightness of the rim and the newness of the nets. Take some shots at both ends. You love this court. Make it your favorite place.*

*Feel the energy in the growing crowd, take a few more shots, and come back to the locker room whenever you're ready. See your teammates all getting ready in their own way. Feel the tension and anticipation in the locker room air. Take a moment quietly to let each other know you're ready and you're a close-knit group. This is what it's all about, this feeling of getting ready to play and compete. This is what fun is all about.*

*Coach takes a moment to bring us together, to remind us to execute our plan and to stay composed and patient against a pressure defense. We will draw them away from the basket and then we'll go back door after we spread them out. We know it will be open and we'll go the basket strongly. We know it will be a physical game, but we are strong, we are positive. We will play our game for forty minutes.*

*Everyone on the bench is ready to play when it's his chance. Everyone must contribute. If you're not on the court pay attention and give support to your teammates.*

*Okay. It's time to go out on the court. We go through warm-ups—lay-ups, passing, shooting. Their fans are cheering loudly for them, ours for us. What a day! What a place to play basketball! Coach (Terry) Holland yells, 'Bring it in,' and we run to the locker room. Everyone* knows the time has come. We're ready, relaxed, peaceful—at ease. We look at one another as our seniors lead us out toward the court.

We hit the court and the crowd goes crazy. We're excited, but we stay as calm as possible, enjoying the situation. TV cameras are everywhere. Photographers are on the court.

There's the opening tip, and the game begins. We're on offense . . . hard cuts, strong picks. They're pressing us. Then—boom!—we throw a backdoor lob to Kenton Edelin for a dunk. The crowd erupts. We're back on defense, playing with focus and intensity. Everyone's communicating with each other. We're all over Uwe Blob, their 7-foot-4-inch center. We watch Steve Alford really closely. A shot goes up. We box out strongly. We're sticking jump shots, making backdoor dunks . . . playing great defense.

We sprint to the locker room at halftime. The score is close. We take care of business. We have a drink. The coaches know we're ready, but they want us to know we must play twenty more minutes to get the win. We get the ball first. We want to start fast. We know Coach (Bobby) Knight loves intensity and will press us even harder.

We stay composed and patient and look for the lob to Othell Wilson instead of Kenton. It works great. He makes a super catch and drops it in the basket. They're frustrated. We know jump shots will open up now. They want to get it inside and can't. The game is in our hands. It will come down to the last seconds, and we excel in fi-

*nal seconds. It's our game plan—keep the score low, control tempo, then win with composure, defense, and good free throw shooting.*

*We're playing our game, not theirs. We're ready for anything they try. Crisp passes. Drawn fouls. Everyone sticking free throws, playing defense, boxing out, rebounding.*

*Now, let's prepare for being behind in the final minutes. We're extending our defense for the first time. They'll be surprised. We're trapping in the half-court corners. We're rested and energetic. We feel quick. We force a turnover and convert. We're making our free throws, and we go to the line in the last seconds, make them, and win.*

*Let's get ready for overtime. We must play another five minutes with complete concentration. We've played a great forty minutes. We play five more. We do it! The crowd floods the court. Everyone celebrates. We're on our way to Seattle.*

*Now slowly open your eyes, clench your fists and very slowly, when you're ready, get up. Go quietly to your room, go to bed and think about these things.*

The next day, Virginia beat Indiana 50–48. The game unfolded in reality much as it had in our visualization exercise. We lost to Houston in overtime in the Final Four. But there is no doubt that the exercises helped the team get as far as it possibly could, much further than the "experts" thought that it could.

You'll notice that we didn't try to imagine Virginia playing a perfect basketball game and blowing Indiana out. We wanted to prepare for a tight game, a game in which the team might trail and have to come back. Your golf preparation should be similar. Imagine yourself coping with all sorts of contingencies. But always imagine yourself doing good things. For instance, you'll want to prepare yourself for the possibility of having to right yourself after a few early bogies. You need not, and should not, force yourself to conjure up the bad swings that lead to those dropped shots. Start your scenario on the fifth tee, when you begin to make the pars and birdies that get you back into contention.

There are many individual variations on a successful visualization exercise. You might see yourself at normal speed, slow speed, or fast speed. Some people emphasize images, and some people emphasize feelings and emotions. Their body tingles as it would when they walk down the last fairway, fighting to win with a calm, clear mind.

But there is one thing all successful visualization exercises have in common. You must concentrate and focus. A superficial, casual effort is not going to help you, any more than a superficial and casual gym workout will make you more fit for golf. The benefits of visualization exercises are commensurate with the effort you give them.

## THOUGHTS TO VISUALIZE BY

Visualization is a path to confidence. It can give you a sense of *déjà vu* in a competitive situation that's new to you.

We all visualize better when we're relaxed.

Visualization works best if it's vivid, detailed, and real.

A superficial, casual effort will not help you.

Take time to visualize success on a regular basis.

Get calm and relaxed before you visualize. Work on imagining the entire sensory experience you want to have.

Visualize yourself coping with difficult situations.

# TWENTY-EIGHT

# HOW WINNING HAPPENS

O   O   O

*Basically, I sought three things from the game—to
compete at it, to improve at it, and to win at it.*
—*Jack Nicklaus*

There are two ways to win in golf. You can win a tournament.
You can win the battle with yourself.

I want my clients to have dreams, even big dreams. When a
player tells me he dreams of winning many, many times, of
racking up major championships, I say, "Great." Those kinds
of dreams are powerful motivations. But I want them to understand that winning tournaments is a matter of both skill
and chance.

I want them to understand that tournament victories happen in all sorts of odd ways, and they have to be ready for all
of them. Very rarely does a player win because for four con-
secutive days he kept striking pure 3-irons to within a few feet
of the flags. More often, it's a matter of figuring out ways to get
the ball in the hole at critical moments even when you're not

hitting it as well as you'd like. I think of Adam Scott at the 2004 Players Championship. I suspect he never dreamed that he'd win a big event like that while hitting his approach to the 72nd green into the water. But he stayed calm, chipped his fourth to the correct tier on the green and holed his ten-footer to win by a shot. He got the job done.

Quite often you win because someone else falters and opens the door for you. Just as often, you play very well and lose to someone who played just a little bit better. I think of Padraig Harrington at the same event Adam Scott won. Padraig played beautifully that week; the birdie putt he sank on the final hole was masterful. He told me afterward how pleased he was that he'd eliminated every other thought from his mind except his target and stroked the putt freely. Indeed, he'd done that throughout the tournament.

Padraig was a winner in another sense, and the only sense that a player can ultimately control. He got his mind in the right place on nearly every shot he played. You can win every time you play golf if you can do that.

It's easy for sportswriters or commentators to deride this idea, to suggest that there's something less than manly about a player who's satisfied to finish second, or tenth, or thirty-fifth if he knows that he did everything he could to perform as well as he could. The writers who push this idea, like to quote Vince Lombardi as saying, "Winning isn't everything; it's the only thing."

I had a cousin named Sal Somma who knew Lombardi, and from him I know the story behind that quotation. Sal played for New York University against Fordham in the era when Lombardi was a member of the offensive line called the Seven

Blocks of Granite. Later, Sal became a high school football coach, one of the best in the history of New York City schools. His teams at New Dorp High School played the single-wing, and they were powerhouses at around the same time Lombardi was a very successful high school coach at St. Cecilia's in Englewood, NJ.

They stayed in touch through the years, even after Lombardi became a legend with the Green Bay Packers and that quote became part of his legend. My cousin asked him about it.

Lombardi said he had first heard the expression from a losing coach at Vanderbilt, Red Saunders. He wasn't sure what Saunders had meant by it. But Lombardi said he had never meant to denigrate another human being about winning or losing a football game. He was talking about making the commitment to winning, the commitment to excellence. He saw winning as an attitude, a state of mind, a level of commitment rather than an end result. He told my cousin that sometimes his teams might lose a game by a touchdown or two, but if he thought the team had made the commitment and given it their best, he would be the first to pat them on the back in the locker room and tell them what a great job they did. On the other hand, there might be times when he felt they were the better team and they lost because they didn't give a full commitment and their best effort. Then, he'd be the first to kick them in the butt and tell them so. The point is that Lombardi was about the commitment to excellence. He wasn't about the final score.

If you make that commitment to excellence and honor it throughout a tournament, then you're a winner in the battle with yourself. You'll also win some of the tournaments.

## THOUGHTS TO WIN BY

**Winning tournaments happens in all sorts of odd ways.**

**A golfer can always win the battle with himself.**

**Make the commitment to win the battle with yourself.
Tournament wins will happen.**

# TWENTY-NINE

# IF YOU PLAY TODAY

O   O   O

*I love championship competition, after all—*
*win or lose.*
*—Bobby Jones*

Back in the introductory chapter, I listed ten things a player must do in every competitive round he plays. To refresh your memory, here they are again:

   I.  **Play to play great. Don't play not to play poorly.**

   II.  **Love the challenge of the day, whatever it may be.**

   III.  **Get out of results and get into process.**

   IV.  **Know that nothing will bother or upset you on the golf course, and you will be in a great state of mind for every shot.**

   V.  **Playing with a feeling that the outcome doesn't matter is almost always preferable to caring too much.**

**VI.  Believe fully in yourself so you can play freely.**

**VII.  See where you want the ball to go before every shot.**

**VIII.  Be decisive, committed, and clear.**

**IX.  Be your own best friend.**

**X.  Love your wedge and your putter.**

I hope by this time that you understand each of these concepts. If you're going out to play golf today, try them. Make observing each of these principles your goal for the round. You'll have fun. You'll shoot the best score you can possibly shoot, given the state of your game today.

I guarantee it.

## ABOUT THE AUTHORS

**Dr. Bob Rotella** is a pioneer in the field of sports psychology and the preeminent counselor to players on the PGA, LPGA and Champions Tours. Among the clients he's worked with are two hall of Famers, Tom Kite and Pat Bradley, as well as Darren Clarke, Padraig Harrington, Billy Mayfair, Davis Love III, and Brad Faxon. Dr. Rotella has counseled teams and coaches in major league baseball, NASCAR and professional basketball. He has been a performance enhancement consultant to numerous major corporations, including Merrill Lynch and Pepsico. He was for twenty years the director of sports psychology at the University of Virginia. He lives in Virginia with his wife, Darlene, and their daughter, Casey.

**Bob Cullen** is a journalist and novelist. In the decade since he began collaborating with Dr. Bob Rotella, his golf handicap has dropped from twenty-one to five.